D0599345

Communication Strategies for Professionals

Second Edition

Jeremy B. Teitelbaum

*California Polytechnic
State University
San Luis Obispo, CA*
Department of Communication Studies

Kendall Hunt
publishing company

First edition title was *Communication Skills for Professionals*.

www.kendallhunt.com
Send all inquiries to:
4050 Westmark Drive
Dubuque, IA   52004-1840

Printed in the United States of America
10 9 8 7 6 5 4 3 2 1

Dedicated to my children:
Gabrielle and Rachel.

Acknowledgement

I would like to express my appreciation to the following for all the help and support in putting together this text. Jill Scala for the advice guidance and insight in the text and accompanying manual. Also Martin Mehl for great thoughts and ideas on the manuscript and offering guidance and insight. Diane Auten for her amazing contribution on presentation technology. Andrea Sanders for giving me fantastic ideas to add to the quality of the material and supporting my publishing of the second edition of the book. Heidi Schultz for help editing and adding some great ideas. A very special thanks to Dr. Frank Forcier for his support and guidance and to the extraordinary team at Kendall Hunt Publishing for their amazing work in editing, proofreading, and layout. And finally, my thanks to Caitlyn Webster for proofreading an early version of the textbook. This all wouldn't be possible without you.

—Jeremy

Contents

A Prologue

The purpose of this textbook is to accompany an introductory course in Communication. This is NOT the complete course. However, it should help you to review information that was begun in class and allow you to further explore in greater detail information that is required, but not discussed.

Students should view the textbook as a supplement. It will not replace the lecture discussions that occur in the classroom. And, as such, it would be impossible to succeed in a course like this by only reading the textbook and not attending lectures.

The book is formatted to leave space in the margins for the reader to take notes. In addition to highlighting sections of interest, the readers should write key words and bullet points in the margins. Don't forget there is a glossary in the back of the book to help you remember key terms. This will allow for ease of studying the reading materials at a later date (e.g., before the final exam).

—Jeremy Teitelbaum
  Summer 2013

Chapter 1

An Introduction

A dog is not considered a good dog because he is a good barker. A man is not considered a good man because he is a good talker.
—Chaung Tzu

Imagine that it is ten years from now. What would the world look like? What would your life be like? You are a college graduate. Maybe you are working in your dream job . . . or you are now very close to it. Think for a moment about the role communication plays in what you do. Do you regularly interact with other people? Who are these people? Are they coworkers? Employees? Your supervisors? Clients? Sub-contractors? Family members? Friends? A significant other? Perhaps all of the above . . . and more. How important is your ability to effectively communicate with all of these people?

Here is a prediction: Your ability to effectively communicate with other human beings will be the single most important determinant to success in everything you do.

Now, that is a serious and powerful statement. But it is true. Effective communication is more important than being skilled at your career. The best architects, business executives, engineers, teachers, forest rangers, scientists, firefighters, politicians, friends, husbands, wives, and parents are those who can communicate with other people. Many college graduates get hired, not because of their G.P.A, not because of their senior projects, not because of the courses they have taken, or the internships they have completed, not even because of the skills they possess, but because of one thing: Their ability to effectively communicate. That's right. If an employer feels you can talk with people from diverse backgrounds, listen to people with different opinions, share your ideas, learn from others, grow in your knowledge and skills, and help people and that organization to succeed, you are ahead of a majority of the competition. It is much easier for an architect to teach a young architect the skills and knowledge of her experience than to teach that new hire to be an effective communicator.

THE HANDSHAKE THAT
SHOOK A NATION

In April of 2013, Microsoft founder and CEO Bill Gates traveled to South Korea and met with that nation's president Park Geunhve. As photographers snapped pictures of the initial greeting, Mr. Gates (assumingly) without realizing it, reached out and shook hands with Ms. Guenhve with an insulting gesture. As is common in many nations, the United States included, proper handshakes can symbolize respect and enthusiasm as well as seal a business deal or sometimes represent peace between two nations. In many Asian nations, handshakes carry numerous customs and traditions of subtle respect, authority, and status. Mr. Gates, who was wearing a jacket and tie, casually shook the President's hand while leaving his left hand in his pants pocket. Although this simple and causal handshake may be quite acceptable in western culture, in South Korea it is considered to be insulting in this situation. Generally in many parts of Asia, a respectful and formal handshake requires the use of both hands. The "single handed shake" is reserved for good friends of the same age or younger. And the hand in the pocket is considered rude and a sign of superiority. While it seems like something small and insignificant, given the status and success of Bill Gates, had it been a mistake made by an average business professional traveling abroad, it could have resulted in the loss of a significant business agreement.

THE TEXT THAT (ALMOST)
UPSET A FRIENDSHIP

Below is a text exchange that took place between myself and my co-author Jill Scala. As you read the exchange, can you see how we had a misunderstanding?

Jeremy: Can you pick me up from the airport at about 1 p.m. today?

Jill: I would usually be able to do it, but today I have crap. Sorry.

Jill: Class.

Jeremy: Ha! I figured.

When I asked Jill to pick me up from the airport, I knew that she was teaching (but didn't remember what time) so it was worth asking. Her reply of having "crap" was either clearly a misspelling of "class" or simply a reference to having "crap" to do. Either way, I knew what she meant. So when she sent me the correction, I replied that I "figured" what she was saying. However, since there is no nonverbal tone in our text messages, my friend assumed that I figured she would not pick me up from the airport and was responding in a sarcastic manner. After making this assumption, she became upset at me for what she perceived was my response to her using a negative and sarcastic tone (she also assumed that I was upset, although I wasn't). Although being sarcastic, rude, or in any way insulting was not my intention, we clearly had a misunderstanding by texting. Needless to say, later that day we had a conversation and were able to resolve the confusion. However, my personal opinion of text messaging is that it is useful for quick exchanges, but can be very detrimental to relationships when used to replace the kind of communication that would be better suited to an actual conversation.

One of my colleagues who teaches communication and emphasizes intercultural communication (see Chapter 2 for a description) is often invited to other countries to conduct trainings for international business executives on how to interact with Americans. Most recently he has been traveling to China to teach students in management classes "proper" communication with Europeans and Americans. It seems that as our economy continues to globalize, there will be an increasing need for better communication between members of diverse cultures and nationalities.

THE KIDS ARE ALL RIGHT

Talking 'bout My Generation

One area of communication problems and conflict in the workplace occurs between members of different generations. Although we can assume this has probably been the case for centuries, this is the first time in American history that we have had such a broad age range and generational differences in the workplace. Older workers are staying longer before they retire, and younger workers are often starting sooner. As many movies will attest to, attitudes about work, family, social life, technology, and communication differ greatly between people in their 20s and people in their 60s. Yet it is quite common for members of each of these generations to work side by side in organizations today. The result can be misunderstandings, communication breakdowns, and occasionally animosity between workers of different ages.

CRITICAL THINKING IN A COMMUNICATION CLASS

Communication and particularly public speaking is required as a lower division, general education prerequisite at most universities worldwide. There are two reasons this course is so important and beneficial. The first and most obvious reason is the need to be able to speak in public, work with groups, interact with diverse people, and share ideas which are directly linked to success in the working world. The more experience and practice we have in this, the better we will be at doing our jobs, and we may even make more money.

However, the second reason is subtler and may not be as obvious to students who are new to college life. It simply comes down to this: Communication (when done well) requires the use of critical thinking, one of the most important skills to have in our highly complex, rapidly changing, often uncertain globalized society. First, let's discuss what it is, then we can further explore why this skill and ability is so valuable to possess.

So what is **critical thinking**? It is just what it sounds like: the ability to think critically. Meaning, to systematically analyze, break-apart, and understand the complexities of thoughts, concepts, and ideas. In other words, it is a method or way of understanding why an argument makes sense (or doesn't), why some evidence is credible, and some is not, or why some solutions to problems will work, and others will not. Most importantly, it is a skill that allows us to express our own ideas to others in ways that will make sense to them (and often influence them to support those ideas).

If we examine the writings of early philosophers in this field, starting with Socrates some 2,500 years ago, and continuing to the 20th century with philosopher, psychologist, and educator John Dewey (1910), we will see that this subject has concerned humankind for quite some time. Even to this day, the state of California has outlined standards of critical thinking that students in high school are expected to meet (see the California Commission on Teacher Credentialing). In fact, amongst university instructors the subject is often discussed and debated at conferences and in the hallways of lecture halls. As a result, many people have different ideas of what it means for students to think critically and furthermore disagree on how that can be assessed by instructors in classroom settings. Yet, even with all of these disagreements and disparaging beliefs about how to measure critical thinking, there seems to be a consensus that it should be a primary learning objective of any effective communication course. As a result, this has led to some common assumptions about what it means to think critically and how that can be evidenced by students in classrooms and measured by instructors assessing student work. Below are the most common definitions and assessments of critical thinking processes.

1. Critical thinking is something that students *can* learn to do and improve with practice. Therefore, critical thinking is a learned skill.

2. Critical thinking involves asking questions, but they have to be good questions. Therefore, critical thinking requires that we look for problems that we were not aware even existed.

3. Before we answer the questions we have to be aware of what information and knowledge we have and do not have (and how to conduct research to find more information). Therefore, critical thinking demands that we seek knowledge.

4. We must understand the ways that we reason (see the chapter on persuasion for a brief list) and we must understand the errors of reasoning (the fallacies in Chapter 11). Therefore, our current understanding of logic and reasoning always limits our critical thinking.

5. We must be able to test our reasoning and conclusions based on a shared upon criteria that may be established prior to beginning but may also be *ex post facto* (after the fact). Therefore, critical thinking is a social process.

6. We cannot hold onto our conclusions so dearly that we refuse to seek alternatives in the face of new information. Therefore, the process of conducting critical thinking is ongoing and never ending.

7. Critical thinking allows us to develop a self-consciousness about our own thinking and reasoning processes. Therefore, critical thinking is a self-reflective process demanding we look inward as well as outward.

8. And finally critical thinking improves our ability to think and reason and provides us opportunities to increase the depth of problems we can analyze and (hopefully) solve. Therefore, critical

thinking builds upon itself to help us think more critically (and makes us "smarter").

So if I were to summarize the above as simply as I could, I would tell students that the best way to show critical thinking is to answer every single possible question of *why* we feel how we feel. Let's try it by answering the following question: Are you having a good day? Why? Now, for each of your reasons why, I am going to ask you again to explain why. This will go on until I truly understand your reasons, or until you are tired of me asking *why* and turn and walk away. Here is my answer to the question: *Jeremy, are you having a good day?*

Yes, I am having a good day.
Why?
Because I have written a lot on this book.
Why?
Because it is taking longer to write than I thought it would and it feels good to accomplish a lot.
Why?
It feels good to accomplish a lot because I know that my publisher is waiting on me to submit the manuscript so that they can have it ready for fall term.
Why?
I don't want to upset my publisher.
Why?
Because they have trusted me to complete this manuscript on time and have given me the opportunity to publish the book.
Why?
Because I do not want them to think I am a failure.
Why?
Because I have struggled with completing other things in the past (my undergraduate degree took seven years) and I don't want anyone to think I am not competent.
Why?
Because I guess I have some insecurities about myself and completing this book will make me feel like I am successful.
Why?
Because I don't want to feel like a failure.
Why?
I think I will have to talk to my therapist and do some deep counseling to address that one. . . .

So you can see that a simple question can be answered at quite a deep analytical level when we attempt to think critically about the question/ answer. Aren't you glad we don't do this on a daily basis (imagine how long the line in the grocery store would be if the clerk wanted to critically analyze every customer's response to "How are you?")?

However, the value and benefits of quality critical thinking should be obvious when we look at questions like: How can we reduce gun violence in America? How can we improve education in our community? How should we allocate our tax resources to benefit as many of us as possible? Or how can we strike a balance with our need for immigration in America and the needs of those already living here?

So you can see why most (if not all) universities require a critical thinking component in their comprehensive undergraduate education, and why employers may be willing to handsomely compensate those who can perform these skills well.

SUMMARY

So, if you are like many students who ask, *why do I need public speaking and communication to earn my degree in (fill in the blank)*, then you should know one thing: We ALL need communication.

REFERENCES

Dewey, J. (1910). *How we think*. New York, NY: Heath.

Chapter 2

What is Communication?

The world has changed. So has the way we communicate. Those who fail to adapt will be left behind. But for those who want to succeed, there is only one secret: YOU ARE THE MESSAGE.
—Roger Ailes

President of CNBC, host of "Straight Forward," and author of "You are the Message."

Key Concepts to Understand
Communication
Messages
Symbols
Transaction
Levels
Model of Communication

There is a difference between good communication and bad communication. Few would argue with that. But, <u>both</u> are still communication. Therefore, this simple point illustrates one of the most complex ideas in the study of communication. Communication, in and of itself, has no value. It is neither good nor bad. It is neither effective nor ineffective. Communication just *is*. In order to study communication, one must put aside any preconceived notions about communication and begin, in a sense, with a blank slate. That is hard to do. After all, most college

students have been communicating (and for the most part rather effectively) for 17 or more years. *We haven't had any problems thus far,* some
will say, so why NOW do we need to study this basic human activity? Be
patient. . . .

Before we can study communication we must define it. Any college student knows this. Perhaps not because of need, but because of
experience. Virtually any introductory college course will begin with a
definition or series of definitions. An introductory course in communication is no different. And, like many disciplines that one studies, there
are multiple explanations, definitions, opinions, and ideas about
what is (and therefore what is NOT) communication. In fact, by some
accounts there are well over 160 different definitions of human
communication.

What did you do this weekend? Did you communicate? How so? In
fact, chances are in any 48-hour period of time (assuming that you didn't
sleep through most of it), you are very likely to have spent more than
half of your time communicating in hundreds of different ways. Did you:

- Send/receive electronic mail
- Watch television
- Have a conversation with a roommate
- Surf the Internet
- Listen to music
- Send and receive text messages
- Talk on a cell phone
- Read a magazine
- Read a billboard while driving
- Instant message a friend
- Post to your social media page
- Video chat with a family member

What do all of these have in common? Certainly they are all forms of
communication, but what is the link? What they all have in common is
this: You are sending and receiving messages in each of these. That's it!
Communication is nothing more, and nothing less than:

THE EXCHANGE OF MESSAGES

So that's it. Communication is the exchange of messages? What about ideas, thoughts, feelings, emotions, and all the rest of the things that we communicate about?

Well the answer is . . . No. Those "things" are what we are communicating **about**, but not communication itself. It is truly impossible for us to ever give another human being our emotions. We cannot take ideas out of our minds and give them to someone. We could never make another person know what we know or feel what we feel. It is impossible.

The best that we can hope for is to find the right words or the right messages to convey our ideas, thoughts, feelings, emotions, and desires to someone else. Then we hope (and occasionally pray) that they "get it." Unfortunately, as we all know so well, often it doesn't work out that way. Sometimes, we find ourselves telling someone: "That's not what I meant." or "You don't understand what I'm saying." But, that's life.

WHAT ARE MESSAGES?

What do we mean when we say that communication is an exchange of messages? Simply put, messages are the words that we use to express whatever it is we are trying to communicate. But, as we all know, sometimes words alone are not enough to communicate. Sometimes we incorporate things like facial expressions, hand gestures, pointing, and emphasis of certain words. So, therefore, to say that messages are words would not be accurate. After all, can we communicate without words at all? Of course!

We constantly receive messages from all around. Do animals send messages then? Well, not exactly. Animals communicate but not with messages. Nor do they use language, nor symbols. Therefore, there are three things that comprise our definition of messages.

Symbols

So, messages are the **symbols** we use to exchange meaning. In plain terms, a symbol is *something that represents something else*. We will discuss symbols in more detail in a later chapter.

Shared Code

In order for a symbol to be used in communication, it must be something that other humans understand. Symbols must be shared in order to understand and exchange meaning. A **shared code** *simply means that we understand what the symbols used to communicate represent*. This does not suggest that the code (or in most cases, language) must be shared identically. For example, you can communicate with someone who doesn't speak English by finding a shared code (you point to things or make hand gestures). Additionally, just because we speak the same language doesn't mean that we share the code. If I said to you, "I'm a little bit pissed, I've got to run to the Lou, and can you spare a fag." you may have no idea what I'm talking about. But the English refer to the toilet as the "Lou," being drunk as "pissed," and a cigarette as a "fag."

Culture

So what then determines if we are sharing the code? The answer lies in our culture. **Culture** means *a group of people who* (among other things) *share the ability to communicate*. Think about how important language is to one's culture. If a Native American nation loses its language (in that people no longer speak it), then there is a part of the history and culture of the people that is lost as well. Language is what ties our culture together.

WHAT IS AN EXCHANGE?

By suggesting that communication is an exchange, we make one important point. Communication is not one-way, but rather it is two-way.

Transaction

An economic transaction involves the exchange of goods or services for something of value (usually money). A communication transaction involves the sending and receiving of messages. Keep in mind that we are talking about messages, not just words. That means anything unspoken can also be included.

Is communication *always* a transaction? For example, can you have a two-way interaction with your television? Perhaps you know someone who tends to yell at the TV set (especially during Raiders football games).

Is this communication? The answer is no. However, is there communication with television? Of course. The ratings you say . . . exactly. To better understand how the television ratings systems work, see the section at the end of this chapter.

Intention

In the basic definition of communication, we are assuming one important factor. That both parties are intentionally communicating. Certainly it can be argued that this is not always the case. In fact, even within the discipline itself, scholars continue to debate the role of intention in the communication transaction. But, for the sake of simplicity in the model described in this textbook, a general assumption of intention will be made. **Intention** means that *all parties have come together with the express purpose of exchanging messages.*

Medium

It may seem obvious, but we still must include a medium or channel in the definition of communication. It would not be possible to communicate without one. A **medium** *is the means by which a message moves between the sender and the receiver.* This includes the airwaves that we use to send our voices, the radio waves used to send radio broadcasts, and the more complex means used to exchange electronic messages.

THE PROCESS OF COMMUNICATION (SEE BERLO, 1960)

The basic process of communication is as follows. Let's imagine we have two people (we will discuss if this applies to one person later). You are the sender and your friend is the receiver. You send a message; your friend receives and processes the message and then gives you feedback. All of this occurs within a particular context and with the inevitable interference of noise (see Figure 2.1).

Sender

Sometimes called the speaker, encoder, or source, this is the person who is doing the talking.

Receiver

Sometimes called the listener, audience, responder, or decoder, this is the person who is doing the listening.

Message

As was discussed earlier, these are the symbols that are moving between the sender and receiver.

Feedback

This is a verbal and/or nonverbal response to the message initiated by the receiver and sent to the sender.

Context

This is the situation in which communication takes place. It can include any of the seven primary contexts or levels (see below).

Noise

This is any interference during communication. It includes not only physical noise, such as a TV or vacuum cleaner, but also emotional noise, such as personal problems, being tired, hungry, biased against the speaker, or not interested.

THE LEVELS OF COMMUNICATION

When we refer to context, we are talking about unique situations that play an important and influential role in communication. As we move through each of the levels, the way we communicate, the types of messages, the people involved, and even the actual words we use change greatly.

Intrapersonal

This is communication within ourselves. There is some debate as to whether or not this is even a true level of communication. Some scholars argue that it is the basic level of all communication. After all, before we can communicate with anyone else, we must communicate with ourselves to formulate and create messages. Generally, this is left to the study of psychology.

Interpersonal

This is communication between two people who have a relationship between each other. It should come as no surprise that this is the largest area of communication being studied by scholars today. Within this level, communication between people involved in long-term relationships (marriage) is the most fruitful area of study. This level is unique because the communication is the "glue" that holds these relationships together. Few who have been in, or observed a marriage would argue that communication is one of, if not THE MOST important determinants to success.

Small Group

Groups are the cornerstones of our society. From work groups, to social groups, and to families, groups are what make us human. What makes a group of people a small group is that they have some common characteristics and communication. (See the chapter detailing communication in small groups). We are generally talking about at least three people and no more than twelve individuals who share some common goals.

Public Speaking

Whether we like it or not, we will have to speak in public. From presentations in the work place, to making a speech at a social group, and to standing up and advocating your beliefs at the local community group, presentations are part of life. This form of communication is very unique in that you have a goal and purpose that you hope to convey to the listeners. A great deal of this textbook will detail how to accomplish that.

Organizational

While small groups may be the cornerstones of society, large organizations are the lifeblood of it. As a result, they often directly and indirectly influence how we communicate. From making rules about what organizational members say to the customer that comes through the door, to developing their own language, modern organizations are truly unique entities when it comes to communication.

Mass Media

As the world has become smaller and technology has advanced, we have moved into the age of global information. We now have twenty-four hour news stations all over the globe, using satellites that allow broadcasters to relay information instantaneously across the world. No one can argue that the mass media, from news to entertainment in film, music, and television, and to advertising, has had a powerful effect on all of society.

Intercultural/Intergroup

In addition to being part of a global society, we live and work in communities that are increasingly diverse. From international organizations, global media, multicultural communities to diverse sexual orientations, and to increasing age gaps, we have experienced an increasing need to communicate with people from all walks of life. This level incorporates all of the above but goes beyond culture. When a doctor speaks with a patient or a nurse, there are barriers (such as status, gender, stereotypes, etc.) that interfere. When police officers speak with community members, there are additional barriers. When teachers and students, politicians and voters all communicate there are major differences in lifestyle and background that can interfere with communication. Scholars who study communication at this level examine how we can overcome these barriers and communicate more effectively.

THE MODEL OF COMMUNICATION

The purpose of the model of communication is to visually represent the process as if seeing it as a snapshot. Obviously, communication is not a snapshot. So the reader must imagine that what you are seeing is a photograph, showing at 1/1000 of a second what happens when we speak. The value in detailing this model is twofold. First, it gives us a way of understanding that communication is a complex process. And second, it gives us a framework for analyzing the process of communication in its complex parts. The rest of this textbook does just that. We look specifically at the sender, the message, and the context. Other courses in communication look at the receiver, feedback, and overcoming noise (see Schramm, 1954).

Figure 2.1 The Model of Communication

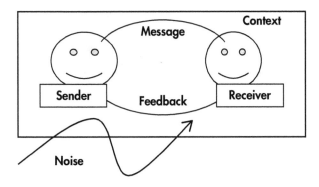

SUMMARY

Most people think of communication as the sharing of ideas, thoughts, feelings, emotions, and beliefs. However, when we communicate, the only things we are sharing are symbols, usually in the form of language. Those symbols represent something common between sender and receiver, and on occasion we do sometimes understand each other's thoughts, feelings, and ideas. However, since we can't just transfer ideas, we are always limited by our use of symbols to communicate. At times this can be very challenging, but when it works well it can also be very rewarding. The rest of this text is dedicated to discovering how we can communicate more effectively.

REFERENCES

Berlo, D. K. (1960). *The process of communication.* New York, NY: Holt, Rinehart and Winston.

Schramm, W. (1954). How communication works. In W. Schramm (Ed.), *The process and effects of communication* (pp. 3–26). Urbana, IL: University of Illinois Press.

Chapter 3

Verbal Communication

Words are, of course, the most powerful drug used by mankind.
—Rudyard Kipling

Key Concepts to Understand
Symbols
Language
Connotative Meaning
Denotative Meaning
Evaluative Role
Potency of Language
Activity of Language
Dynamic Language
Static Language
Euphemisms

In the 1994 film *Nell*, starring Jodie Foster, a young woman is discovered by a psychologist (played by Liam Neeson) after having lived much of her life in the isolation of her mountain cabin. The woman was raised by a deaf and mute mother and has learned her own form of communication. She uses abstract sounds and gestures as expression instead of speaking with words and language. We later find out that she is clearly capable of speech, but being raised and socialized by a mother who could not communicate with words, Nell never learned to speak. This story illustrates the debate among communication scholars as to the origins of language. Although Nell cannot communicate using traditional language, she (and perhaps her mother as well) has created a unique "language" of sorts that is used to communicate. This brings up the important question: Does our use of communication and language stem from nature (we are born with the need) or nurture (we learn to communicate from social interaction)? Recognize that we are not debating the learning and use of any particular languages, per say.

Some years ago in China, women were often socialized into roles subservient to men and thus not allowed to read or write. However, some of these women went so far as to create their very own language using visual symbols. They incorporated these symbols into blankets that they made and "sent" them as letters to friends (Chu, 2001). Perhaps the need to use language to communicate is far deeper than the way we are raised and socialized.

This chapter will examine the various ways that we use symbols to communicate and exchange meaning. We will answer the question: **How** do we exchange messages?

WHAT DOES IT MEAN TO COMMUNICATE SYMBOLICALLY?

As you remember from the previous chapter, a symbol is something that represents something else. In communication we are talking about letters, words, and in general language. But what does it mean to communicate with symbols?

Think for a moment about how most animals communicate. First, how do they learn their forms of communication? Most scientists would agree that animals are born with the ability to make the sounds they use to communicate. Dogs don't have to be taught by their parents to *woof*. Cows do not need to learn to *moo*. Nor do cats need much training to "say" *meow*. That is because those sounds are not symbolic. A dog's bark is not the translation of some other meaning. Children's movies aside, animals do not speak in the ways that humans speak.

In order to communicate with symbols, several things must occur. First, we ourselves must know the symbols we want to use to send a message. Second, we must choose a symbol or set of symbols that we think the receiver will understand. Then we must "give" those symbols to the other party. And they must share the meaning of those symbols with us, so that they can understand. In theory, this sounds easy. As we all know, it is not.

Let's work backwards here. Given all of the thoughts, feelings, emotions, opinions, beliefs, views, attitudes, and ideas humans can have, in English we may have in the neighborhood of 50,000 words that we regularly use (and that still suggests someone who has a fairly large vocabulary). All of those words are based on 26 letters. Not only do we, the speaker, need to know the meaning of these symbols, but so too must the receiver. And if either one of us understands the meaning of these differently; we are unlikely to accurately exchange meaning. Now, is it any wonder that we often have to explain ourselves to another person?

So, to **communicate symbolically** means that instead of using biological sounds (grunts, crying, etc.), we use symbols. Those symbols are primarily letters, words, and language. It is that language that is exchanged in messages, in an effort to exchange meaning. In all reality, meaning is not always exchanged accurately when we communicate. Perhaps right now, you understand the words that you are reading differently than a classmate, and you both understand them differently than the author intended.

Moe Keale performed at Whittier College in Whittier, California, on three occasions. At the end of each concert, Moe told all of us the meaning of **Aloha**. Moe said that Pilahi Paki, a teacher of Hawaiian culture said, "In the next millennium the world would turn to Hawaii as they search for world peace because Hawaii has the key . . . *and that key is ALOHA!*"

Aloha means: kindness, expressed with tenderness; unity, expressed with harmony; agreeable, expressed with pleasantness; humility, expressed with modesty; and patience, expressed through perseverance.

And you thought it meant **Hello**!

Adapted from www.alohajoe.com. Accessed December 22, 2005.

WHAT IS LANGUAGE?

According to the University of Michigan, there are over 2,796 languages in the world today! What is the one thing they all have in common? They are all symbolic. **Language** *is a set of symbols, signs, codes, and rules used to exchange meaning.*

First, let's take a very brief look at the history of language. Most scholars agree that languages were spoken long before they were written. There is evidence of this today. Many languages have no written form. For example, the Chumash Indians, locals on the central coast of California, have a language that is entirely spoken and not written. However, in recent years people have begun to create a written version of the language in an effort to teach it to others, but it should come as no surprise that they are using English letters to phonetically sound out the spoken words. Furthermore, some languages are written and not spoken, such as computer programming languages, and the works of J. R. R. Tolkien. However, most communication scholars are interested in modern language and modern communication and thus examine both written and spoken languages. Languages tend to evolve over time with use. We can trace the roots of language back to earlier forms and older languages. But what we see is that language is inextricably tied to human beings. And humans are in turn tied to our languages.

HOW DO WE COMMUNICATE WITH LANGUAGE?

There are two basic functions that language serves in communication (McKerrow, et al., 2000). The **referential** function of language means *that we use it to refer to or point to things with labels*. For example, humans tend to name things. There are few mountains without names. Give a child a doll, and she will probably name it. After my second daughter was born, her mother and I were still in disagreement over her name. Should she be Rachel Sophia or Sophia Rachel? The nurses at the hospital began insisting that we come up with her name. It may seem strange to have a child without a name, but that was the case for two days. Although we were still in some disagreement, the nurses decided that they could wait no longer and would need to type up a birth certificate right away. We were told that we MUST tell them the name of the baby or they would not let us leave the hospital. Her name is Rachel Sophia Teitelbaum.

The second function of language is the **relational** function. We use language *to establish and maintain our relationships*. Have you ever had a friend who complained that you had not spoken to him/her for a long time? For many of us, having a relationship with another person means we communicate with them on a regular basis. Language, and more specifically word choice, becomes an influential part of any relationship. In turn, the relationship influences the language. After how many months (if ever) of dating is it appropriate to call someone "honey"?

This influences our cultures as well. Language influences our culture, as does our culture influence language.

> According to the news program *60 Minutes*, the Moken people of Southeast Asia don't know how old they are . . . this is because, "Time is not the same concept as we have. You can't say for instance, 'When.' [The word when] doesn't exist in Moken language."

The Meaning of Words

How do we get the meaning of words? The answer is not the dictionary. The role of the dictionary is to illustrate how words are used (Hayakawa, 1982). Certainly we learn the meaning of words as we grow up *(shared knowledge)*. But, oftentimes there can be more than one definition. As such, we must agree on the meaning with others. However, usually that requires that we look to the context to correctly understand the meaning. How often do people say, "You took what I said out of context." in an effort to clarify understanding? Finally, the relationship between speaker and listener influences meaning as well. Words that may be offensive between two friends may be quite acceptable between another two friends.

Two researchers in the 1930s developed a model to explain how humans communicate using symbols and thus are able to exchange meaning. Ogden & Richards (1946) called the model the "Triangle of Meaning." They argue that humans attach meaning to symbols in three ways. If a friend said to you the word "cat," would you know what she meant? Chances are you would only if it was used in a sentence. Imagine she says, "I have a new cat." Now, is that clear? Is she talking about an animal or a tractor? If she said cat, we may not know. What would you do . . . ask? After she clarifies for you it was an animal, would you know exactly what she meant? Chances are you would not.

The Types of Meaning

This illustrates to us that there are two different types of meaning in words. The **denotative** meaning refers to *the formal (often called dictionary) definition*. This is the more common definition, but doesn't take into account the general or popular use of a word. The **connotative** meaning refers to *the way a word makes people feel and the emotional* *attachment people place on the meaning of words.* Think of common slang words as an example. Sometime look up the denotative definition of one of the slang terms that is used by college students today. Examine the difference in the formal definition and the common usage. You may be surprised to learn there is little if any connection between the two. Would you feel any different if your bank referred to you as a client rather than a customer? Or, how would you feel if a real estate agent called you a customer rather than a client?

THE ROLE OF LANGUAGE

Given what has been said about language thus far, it should not be surprising to hear the following. Language is three-dimensional. It is deeply rooted in the human spirit. It is deeply connected to the human psyche. It is deeply intertwined with our humanity. As a result, language is not something that is static, but something that is active; it grows, changes, and develops just as human society does.

The Evaluative Function of Language

Words can be used in ways that are **positive, negative,** or **neutral**. Imagine you have just seen a movie that you enjoyed greatly. What are some positive words to describe it? "Great, terrific, outstanding, amazing, fabulous, brilliant."

The Potency of Words

Words can be **strong** or **weak**. If you dislike someone, you can say: I *dislike* you or I *hate* you. "Hate" is a strong word. Weak words tend to be somewhat ambivalent. If your grandmother asks you, "How did you like the dinner I cooked for you?" and you respond with it was "OK," "not bad," "so-so," or "ehhhh," you may regret those words on your birthday when she sends you only a $1.00 bill.

The Activity of Words

It may seem very unusual to think of words as having activity, as if they can leap off the page. But metaphorically, they can. Words can be **dynamic** or **static**. Think of the reviews (usually those written by the marketing department) of a potentially blockbuster movie. The language used is often very dynamic. Here are three reviews of the movie *King Kong*:

> ". . . a magnificent entertainment." Roger Ebert of the Chicago Sun-Times

> ". . . gargantuan, mightily entertaining . . ." A. O. Scott of the New York Times

> ". . . the jaw-dropping, eye-popping, heart-stopping movie epic we've been waiting for all year." Peter Travers of Rolling Stone

Those are all excellent examples of dynamic language. Notice how the words sound as if they are jumping off the page at you. Another example of dynamic language is the speech *I Have a Dream* by Martin Luther King, Jr. (see below). Notice that most of this emotion refers to the connotative meanings of words.

PUTTING IT ALL TOGETHER

Eventually, members of a culture attach such powerful connotative meanings to words that they can take on a life of their own. Terms can become so negative that we begin to avoid using them. Or they can become so positive and overused that the meaning becomes meaningless to us. One example of a negative word lately is *employee*. The connotative meaning of employee has become so negative that many organizations today no longer call the people who work their *employees*. They instead use terms like: *associate* (Wal-Mart), *partner* (Starbucks), or *team member* (Target). If words become so negative that it is emotionally painful to say, we develop and use euphemisms instead. Politicians have picked up on this and begin to throw terms around with little if any explanation as to what they mean when they use them. No one running for office is anything but "tough on crime," "for family values," or "strong on education" because those words tell us little or nothing about any real policy issues.

Perhaps the word in the English language with the most euphemisms is *death*. Look online for websites that list euphemisms for this powerful word.

SUMMARY

When we communicate, we are exchanging symbols that represent something to the users. As we have discussed, we really aren't exchanging thoughts, feelings, or ideas. The most common symbols we use to communicate are language. While words often have universal meanings among users (those who speak the language), they can also mean different things to different people. It is no wonder sometimes communicating can be very challenging.

REFERENCES

Chu, H. (2001, November 23). The secret is out: China's mother tongue is dying. *Los Angeles Times*, p. A10.

Hayakawa, S. I. (1982). Contexts. In C. J. Boltz & D. U. Seyler (Eds.), *Language power* (pp. 23–34). New York, NY: Random House.

McKerrow, R. E., Gronbeck, B. E., Ehninger, D., & Monroe, A. H. (2000). *Principles and types of speech communication, 14.* New York, NY: Longman.

Ogden, C. K., & Richards, I. A. (1946). *The meaning of meaning: A study of the influence of language upon thought and of the science of symbolism, 8.* New York, NY: Harcourt, Brace & World.

Chapter 4

Nonverbal Communication

It happened once that a youth and a maiden beheld each other in a public assembly for the first time . . . The youth gazed with great delight upon the beautiful face until he caught the maiden's eye . . . The mysterious communication that is established across a house between two entire strangers, by this means moves all the springs of wonder.
—Ralph Waldo Emerson

Key Concepts to Understand

Nonverbal Communication
Clothing
Artifacts
Kinesics
Facial Expressions
Occulesics
Paralanguage
Haptics
Proxemics
Chronemics
Monochronic/Polychronic

Perhaps more so than any area of communication, nonverbal body language has received more attention and more misinformation than anything else. A search of books on body language at **Amazon.com** yields over 1,600 books on the subject. The sad truth is that a great amount of information in these books is inaccurate, much is flat out wrong, and some is just plain bull-crap. So what do we "know" about nonverbal communication? This chapter will examine the facts.

NONVERBAL COMMUNICATION DEFINED

In the previous chapter we defined verbal communication in several ways. Language and symbols are the means by which we communicate verbally. So what then is the **nonverbal** aspect of communication? In the simplest forms, nonverbal communication is everything else. More formally, *it is the messages that people exchange beyond verbal communication.* Language is NOT nonverbal communication. Do not make the mistake of translating the term literally. Instead, focus on the connotative definition. Therefore, sign language is NOT nonverbal communication. Like any language it is a form of verbal communication. Watch someone signing and you will see they use the same nonverbal communication as someone speaking. Facial expressions, body language, and gestures are all just as important in sign language as in spoken languages. In fact they may be more important since American Sign Language has fewer words (signs) than spoken English. As a result, the context and body language (e.g., nonverbals) become even more important in sharing meaning.

Role/Importance

As anyone who has ever used electronic communication (e.g., email or instant messaging) knows, communication without nonverbal messages is very difficult. In fact, it is so difficult that online chatters invented symbols to represent nonverbal expressions. The signs "LOL" (laughing out loud), ":)" (meaning a smile), "LMAO" (laughing my a$$ off), and others show that in order to communicate we **need** nonverbal communication.

The Trouble with Nonverbal Messages

Nonverbal communication is much more ambiguous than verbal communication. There is no convention as to what nonverbal cues mean. We really have no way of translating a nonverbal message. With verbal communication we have more options. If we don't know what a word means, we can look it up in the dictionary as a starting point. But if we don't know what a gesture means, our first option is to communicate verbally. As a result, more of our misunderstandings are probably related to nonverbal communication than verbal communication. To add to the problems, although some nonverbal messages are entirely intentional, much of them are not. We do not always know and have control over the expression our face makes when we see or hear something astonishing. And if we do try to control our expressions, we may be more confusing to another than if we just let it go naturally. However, as a receiver of nonverbal messages, we tend to assume intention. Have you ever said to someone, "What do you mean by that (arm cross, or facial expression)?" Only to have them respond in sheer confusion, honestly having no idea what message you just received. If you were telling your significant other about an amazing day you had, and they yawn in the middle of your conversation, would you ask, "Am I boring you?" Despite numerous books, articles, workshops, and coaches (see the movie *Hitch* starring Will Smith), there are no hard and fast rules to decoding the "true" meaning of body language, facial expressions, or most nonverbal communication. However, there are some generalizations we can make. And that is what we will do for the rest of this chapter.

Clothing

In March of 2005, Michael Jackson arrived at the Santa Barbara County Courthouse wearing a sport coat and a pair of pajama bottoms. The result . . . Judge Melville said that Jackson's clothing were an insult to the court and threatened to throw Michael in jail! We all know how important clothing is to a job interview or court appointment. But did you know that more so than anything else, clothing is used to identify our culture, religion, and personality?

Can you tell if someone is a serious surfer or skateboarder by the way they are dressed? Can you tell the type of music someone listens to by the clothes they wear? Sometimes we can.

How important is the brand name of your clothes? To some people this sends a very powerful message. And it is not unusual for people to look specifically at the brand names of our clothing. As a graduate student at a conference in San Diego, I learned this firsthand. Some students from another university had heard a presentation by my advisor. They asked me if my advisor was the "guy in the Armani suit"? (Giorgio Armani is a successful fashion designer and his company is quite popular among celebrities and the wealthy.) This simple statement said a great deal about this person and implied he was not only well-dressed but was quite financially successful.

Artifacts

Jewelry is an example of one of the most communicative artifacts in western culture. What is the primary symbol of marriage? The wedding ring worn on the "ring finger" of the left hand. What other cultural symbols do you use to communicate? Does the brand of a person's watch communicate anything to you?

One of the more interesting examples of artifacts in American culture is the automobile. See if you can pair up the car with the person below:

Volvo Station Wagon	Doctor
BMW 325 Sports Coupe	Nonprofit Manager
Audi All-Wheel Drive Sedan	Church Pastor
Mercedes Coupe	Auto Body Painter
Jaguar Convertible	Disc Jockey
Lincoln Navigator	Lawyer
Dodge SUV	College Professor
Toyota Minivan	Police Officer
Ford 4x4 Pickup	UCLA College Student
Subaru Station Wagon	Stay-at-Home Mom
Harley-Davidson Motorcycle	General Contractor

My guess is that you can match up quite a few of these. And if you consider this to be stereotyping, you are right. It is. But do people judge us based on the cars we drive? Of course they do. And for what it's worth, I know one of each of the above individuals who drive (or drove) the above cars (see the end of the chapter).

Another fascinating example of artifacts is the use of body piercing and tattoos. In some cultures, these are used to communicate things like status, age, and accomplishments. According to the University of New Mexico website: "Body piercing is at least 3,400 years old. Egyptian pharaohs pierced their navels, ancient Mayans pierced their faces and genitals, and Roman military officers pierced their nipples, onto which they fastened their heavy capes." Tattoos are symbols that can be used as direct (such as words and names) and indirect communication (such as graphics and pictures). You have probably seen tattoos of objects, animals, people, and corporate logos (Harley-Davidson seems to be quite popular, but I've seen Ford, Chevy, Honda, Ferrari, Playboy, and even the John Deere logo).

The Study of Kinesics

Kinesics *is the study of body language as a form of communication.* This is one of the areas of nonverbal communication that has been studied extensively but is still quite unknown. There is also a tremendous amount of disagreement over the ways in which we use body language. Perhaps the biggest myth around body language is that there exists some hidden "language" of the body, and once understood, all of the secrets of communication would be revealed. Nothing could be further from the truth. As DeFleur, Kearney, & Plax (1998) explain: "This implies that you can't tell what speakers really mean by what they say with words, instead intentions must be read in what the speakers communicate nonverbally. Nothing could be further from the truth." What effective communicators should understand about body language is this: *It is an important part of communication.* By arming ourselves with understanding and knowledge of the ways that we use body language in everyday communication, we can be more effective speakers and listeners.

There are four broad categories of body language that have been studied extensively. Those are facial expressions, the eyes, touch, and the use of physical space.

Gestures
There are five different ways that we use gestures. A **gesture** *is a form of body movement that communicates a message.*

1. Emblems. These are gestures that have a direct verbal translation, such as the middle finger, the "OK" symbol, or the thumbs-up.

2. Illustrators. Hand and/or arm movements the show or reinforce meaning. Say "the fish was this big," while holding your hands up in the air about 12 inches apart, and your listener can see the size of the one that got away.

3. Regulators. These control and influence a conversation. Raising your hand and motioning to a friend that you want to say something (not in the way you do in class, but in a more personal and social way). Even just leaning forward with a facial expression can signify that you want someone to stop talking and you have something to say.

4. Adapters. These tend to be unintentional hand, arms, leg, and body movements. If you are tired you may rub your eyes and stretch your arms. If you are waiting for someone you may start biting your nails, chewing on a pen, or tapping your fingers.

5. Affect Displays. These are unintentional and emotional expressions that we generally have little or no control over. If someone says something hurtful, we may cry. Some people will begin to laugh when very nervous during a speech. If we attend a funeral and people are crying, the message we receive is that people feel sadness.

Facial Expressions

We use facial expression intentionally as well as without even knowing we are making them. One of the leading researchers on facial expression, Paul Eckman claims that our face is capable of nearly 10,000 distinct expressions (1976, 1982). Whether or not that is accurate, it is clear that we often communicate a great deal of information without saying a word. However, there are four primary ways that we use facial expressions that convey meaning.

Intensification. Without even realizing it, we can oftentimes show a great deal of emotion in our faces. Whether it is excitement, sorrow, anger, disappointment, or passion. We intensify *what we feel by letting (or sometimes without even knowing or controlling it) our faces show those feelings*. Young children occasionally will intensify their distress at being hurt when they want some extra attention. Parents occasionally use this tactic to make them feel that we are terribly concerned and worried by their pain ("Oh, what's the matter sweetie . . . did you get an owchy?").

De-intensification. This is the opposite of intensification. *Here we attempt to downplay our facial expression to show less of what we are feeling or thinking*. I recently had to do this when my grandmother was telling me a story that got a little too graphic for a grandmother. Despite my jaw having just dropped to the floor, I attempted to remain cool and look as if I wasn't just shocked by what I had heard this 89-year-old lady tell me.

Neutralization. *This is the "poker face."* Phil Helmuth, a world-champion professional poker player, usually wears sunglasses and a hat while playing the game. This way people cannot "read" his face. We often respond to things people say to us with our poker face. Sometimes we are surprised by what someone said, but we don't want to let on. I recently visited friends who have a two year old who was doing his cookie monster impression while eating. The food went everywhere and he was making a mess. His parents felt that he was doing this to get attention and however funny and cute it was, his parents didn't want to encourage the behavior, so we had to refrain from laughing and continue on with business as normal.

Masking. *This is when we attempt to cover or change our facial expressions for something that is appropriate to the context.* What is different about masking and de-intensification or neutralization is here we actually attempt to "cover-up" our facial expressions. We don't stop at downplaying our emotions; we actually fake it. If you have ever laughed at a really bad joke—just to be nice—you have used this technique.

Occulesics

Occulesics *is the study of the eyes as a form of communication.* As the old cliché goes, the eyes are the window to the soul. If this is true, we must believe it because we feel that the eyes can communicate a great deal of information, emotion, feeling, and honesty.

Can a look or a glance send you a message? Have you ever been in a public place and made eye contact with a stranger across the room? If so, you know that you now have two options. (1) Look away quickly. (2) Allow the eye contact to continue. Assuming you would be open to knowing this stranger, you opt for number two. But how long do you allow the eye contact to continue? Certainly there are no rules on this, but we all know the feeling of having someone across the room stare at us. It is a very uncomfortable feeling to have someone we don't know look at us. Especially when we have "caught" them looking and they still do it. So, if you want to know this stranger across the room, you hold the eye contact for a second or two and then look away. Don't stare . . . or you will freak them out!

Another interesting area of the study of the eyes relates to deception. It should come as no surprise that there are hundreds of books, articles, and theories about how to tell if someone is lying just by look-ing at their body language. The problem is that there are no hidden se-crets to detecting deception in another. Despite all of these myths, there seems to be a generalized acceptance of much of these notions that lack of eye contact signifies important messages. As a result, one of the biggest criticisms of new speakers is a failure to make eye contact. This tends to be the first thing audience members notice about a speaker, and one of the biggest things that affects them. This has led to some simple "norms" on what speakers should and should not do and will be discussed in the section on public speaking.

Haptics

Haptics *is the study of touch as a form of communication.* The ultimate dilemma for the single person: When meeting a new person (of poten-tial romantic interest), should I reach out and shake his/her hand, hug them, or do nothing? No matter what choice you make, it will communi-cate a potentially strong message.

Touch is one of the most important forms of communication be-tween human beings. There is a great deal of research looking at how touch influences our health and well being, growth and development, attraction, and even success in business.

How comfortable are YOU with touching others and being touched? Take the Touch Apprehension Measure (search for it online) and see where you fit in. I grew up in a family and with a social group who hug everyone. When I go home to visit them, such as during the holidays, everyone hugs me. As a result, I'm a "hugger" more than a "shaker" (a line from the TV show *Home Improvement* starring Tim Allen).

Proxemics

Proxemics *is the study of the communication of space and distance.* One of my favorite episodes of the television sitcom *Seinfeld* is the Close Talker episode played by Judge Rheinhold (look it up online). We have all known someone like that, and we all have our own comfort levels with how we use our personal space. This is the area of proxemics known as **Physical Space**. *It refers to how we use the space around our bodies.* Obviously at times when a close friend or loved one invades our space, we don't mind. But when it's someone we don't know . . . it can be very uncomfortable.

Anthropologist Edward T. Hall (1959) came up with a generaliza-tion about how most of us use the personal bubble of space around our body. He suggested that we have four zones of personal space.

1. Intimate Zone. From 0–18 inches. Reserved for close friends.
2. Personal Zone. From 18 inches to 4 feet. Reserved for people we know.
3. Social Zone. From 4 feet to about 8 feet. Open to strangers *if needed.*
4. Public Zone. Beyond 8 feet. Where we prefer to keep strangers.

If you have ever traveled outside of the US, you have experienced how different these levels are within different cultures. Many people in parts of the world are much more accustomed to being very close to strangers. Even within our own cultures we find differences. Researchers have found that gender, age, social status, and cultural background all strongly influence the use of personal space.

In addition to physical space, we use **territory** as a form of communication. *This refers to how we use our surroundings.* Think of the first thing that you did when you moved into your new dorm room or apartment to make the space feel like your own. Did you hang up posters, place pictures of friends and family around, move furniture . . . or just put your stuff on one of the bunks to "claim" it as your own? The size of one's desk or office can be an important measure of success to some organizational workers. Unwritten rules develop around territory. For example, in some situations it may be unacceptable to enter a superior's office without asking or knocking first. In some organizations they brag about an "open door policy," meaning you can walk in anytime. Do you have a certain shelf in the refrigerator? Do you sit in the same desk in any of your classes? Do you get angry if you come home and find your roommate's friends sitting on your bed? We value our territory like animals that claim theirs; we will often "mark" our territory.

Our body language can communicate messages in four ways. It can **complement** the things that we say by adding emphasis, feeling, and meaning to our verbal communication. Body language can also **regulate** verbal communication. Raising our hand can get an entire room of people to stop talking and listen to you. A father's glance can get three young children to stop fighting and sit quietly in the back seat of a car. Body language can occasionally **substitute** for verbal communication. With a slight lean of the head, stretch of the arms, or smile or wink, we can "say" more than any words could ever. And occasionally our body language can **contradict** what was spoken verbally. When this happens, listeners are much more likely to believe the messages they associate with our body language than what we have said.

As we all know, an important part of communication is body language. However, there are many other forms of communication as well. Much of nonverbal communication extends beyond the body and involves the way individuals and cultures use their environment as well.

Chronemics. Remember the example from the previous chapter about the Moken people of Southeast Asia? Can you imagine not knowing how old you are? But that is the case for many people in many parts of the world. Time just doesn't matter in some cultures in the same way that it does in our own culture. Chronemics is the study of how members of a culture use time to exchange messages. Basically, we can narrow down most cultures into one of two categories (Hall, 1959).

Monochronic. This is a culture that views time as being very linear. People tend to place great importance on the value of time. You will hear phrases such as "time is money," "don't waste time," "if you aren't 15 minutes early, you're late," and "let's get down to business." The focus is on the clock, as in the numerical value of time. For example, they value the amount of time something takes (or doesn't take), but not the quality of time. If someone invited you over for dinner at 6:00 p.m. and you were more than 30 minutes late, they would probably be quite offended. Does this describe the United States to you?

Polychronic. This is a culture that doesn't place emphasis on the clock. Literally as in people don't wear watches and they don't care if they are late. They don't stress over it either. If you were invited to a party and asked what time you should arrive, they just might say: anytime, or dinnertime, or whenever. If you showed up for dinner at 10:00 p.m., they would still feed you. In my experience, people from Mexico, Polynesia, and the Philippines are much more Polychronic than Americans.

Who Drives What?

How did you do? In the box on the next page are the types of cars and the occupations of 11 people I have known. Notice how some of the cars that they drive might be called "typical" given their chosen occupations.

SUMMARY

Despite all the myths about nonverbal communication, it is still an important and often misunderstood component of the exchange of messages. While it does not occur separately from verbal communication, as listeners we often focus on it in isolation form language. Researchers and authors may not agree on what the "hidden" meanings of body language truly are, but what we all can agree on is the opportunity to continue to study and understand more about nonverbal communication.

REFERENCES

DeFleur, M. L., Kearney, P., & Plax, T. G. (1998). *Fundamentals of human communication* (2nd ed.). Mountain View, CA: Mayfield.

Eckman, P. (1976). *Pictures of facial affect*. Palo Alto, CA: Consulting Psychologists Press.

Eckman, P. (1982). *Emotion in the human face*. New York, NY: Cambridge University Press.

Hall, E. T. (1959). *The silent language*. Garden City, NY: Doubleday.

Volvo Station Wagon—Professor
BMW 325 Sports Coupe—UCLA College Student
Audi All-Wheel Drive Sedan—Nonprofit Manager
Mercedes Coupe—Lawyer
Jaguar Convertible—Doctor
Lincoln Navigator—Disc Jockey
Dodge SUV—Police Officer
Toyota Minivan—Mom
Ford 4x4 Pickup—Contractor
Subaru Station Wagon—Pastor
Harley-Davidson Motorcycle—Auto Body Painter

Chapter 5

Effective Listening

Courage is what it takes to stand up and speak;
Courage is also what it takes to sit down and listen.
—(attributed to) Winston Churchill

Key Concepts to Understand
Difference between Listening vs. Hearing
Active vs. Passive Listening
Types of Listening
Responding when Listening

College students spend a great deal of time listening to lectures, classmates, friends, music, television shows, online videos, and sometimes parents. However, we often take this process for granted. In fact, chances are if you recorded your average day, you would spend more time listening than speaking. Yet, few people will ever take a class on the subject of listening, while most college students are now required to take a class on speaking. As a result, many people aren't very good at listening to others.

LISTENING VS. HEARING

There is the difference between listening and hearing. When we are **hearing** something, we are engaging in a physiological process of receiving noise that is interacting with our eardrums and influencing our

39

brains to respond. In fact, we are constantly listening at all times throughout the day. Think about walking through your campus and the noises you are hearing all around you. You may hear cars driving by or bicycles riding past you. There are probably people walking by and talking to each other or on cell phones. There may be birds singing in the trees above you. Perhaps there is construction noise as you pass buildings being worked on. And don't forget the internal dialogue that is going on inside of your own mind. One way that our brains respond to the listening can be to "tune it out." In reality, everything we hear doesn't affect us consciously.

A great example of how we are constantly hearing but not always listening happened to me several weeks ago as I was walking through campus. While thinking about all the things I needed to do and trying to tune out the incredible noise of the construction equipment that was building our new science building, I heard a young lady in the distance. At first it didn't even register in my mind because I thought someone was laughing. But, as I got a little closer, I realized it wasn't laughter but crying. Suddenly I found myself completely focused on this young lady who was talking on a cell phone and crying. I began to wonder what was wrong and thought about whom she was speaking to. Before I knew it, I was completely focused on what was going on with this person and had stopped thinking at all about the construction noise, what I had to do that day, or anything else for that matter. With my full attention given to her, I began eavesdropping on her conversation. It seemed she was very stressed out about the work she had due in her classes and was not going to be able to go home to visit her mother for some sort of event that was planned in the near future. Clearly this had caused an emotional response in her that had led to tears. I immediately began thinking about how I could relate to that situation, not only when I was a student, but even now as an instructor.

As you can see, my hearing was quickly converted to listening intently as the sounds became something of interest to my conscious mind. This illustrates the difference between hearing and listening.

So *listening* is the act of hearing and then processing (thinking about) and responding to messages (noise). There are several components to listening that go beyond hearing. Listening involves *processing*, which is an attempt to understand the meaning of the noises we are hearing. It also involves *responding* to those messages. This may include saying something or nothing because it is a conscious process of interacting with a message. So, choosing to ignore the message is a form of responding.

Interference with Listening

We have already discussed the role of noise in the model of communication. Noise is something that interferes with our ability to exchange messages and can never truly be "turned off." However, there are many types of noise that can make it difficult to listen to communication. Let's examine the physical, social, physiological, and psychological types of noise that can interfere with listening.

Physical Noise

This can include anything that interferes with *hearing* and thus makes it difficult to listen. An example would be a television set turned on too loud, a vacuum cleaner in the background, construction noise in the distance, and so on. This can also include the volume being turned down too low on your television set or a speaker who isn't speaking loud enough for you to hear her from where you are sitting in the audience. Our brains are remarkably effective at "tuning out" much of these distractions when we truly want to focus on something, and yet also quite good at becoming a distraction (usually when we aren't interested). Have you recently been sitting in class and found yourself a little bored and noticed that you are listening to the noises outside the classroom and not paying attention to your lecture? I think we have all had that experience.

Social Noise

This is an idea that I discovered after taking several sociology courses in college and it seems to be making its way into popular culture recently and perhaps academic literature in the near future. This stems from the notion that in public situations we have certain social norms about communication and as a result are often limited by how much we are able to focus on while listening. Some examples of social noise might be people laughing out loud during a movie screening or people talking loudly in a public place. But in many ways this is more complex as our use of personal media and social media is on the rise. Do you ever feel overwhelmed with trying to keep track of your Facebook, Twitter, Instagram, text messages, email, and voicemail? If so, then you are being bombarded with the 21st century version of social noise.

Physiological Noise

Our physiological processes can often interfere with our ability to listen to someone or something. Have you ever been so tired at night while having a deep conversation with a friend that you just couldn't stay awake and participate? Have you ever been so hungry in class that you would swear you could hear your stomach growling and just couldn't focus on the lecture material? Have you ever found yourself trying to talk to someone who clearly has had too much to drink . . . ? If you can relate to any of those, then you have been a "victim" of physiological noise interfering with listening abilities.

Psychological Noise

This type of noise refers to the emotional attitudes and beliefs that we all carry with us that can occasionally interfere with the ability to listen to someone else. Examples can include the biases or stereotypes we have about people, such as assumptions we make about older adults being unable to hear us unless we raise our voices, talk slowly, and enunciate our words clearly. Have you ever noticed you were tuning someone out because they were much older than you? Other examples include the opinions we have about political, religious, and cultural groups. If you went to hear a political speech on a subject that you were interested in but was being delivered by a member of your opposing political party, you may have some preconceived notions, biases, and opinions about that person simply because of his political affiliation. As a result, you may occasionally tune out that person and choose to disregard some or most of what they say. Even language barriers can fit into this category. Although a strong accent is a type of physical noise, it is impossible for us to turn off the opinions we have of people who are different than we are, especially speakers of other languages. The result is often more than just a language barrier, but a cultural barrier that interferes with listening.

The point of understanding the listening barriers is to recognize that they are almost always there. They interfere with our ability to speak and to listen to others unless we make a conscious effort to minimize them and do our best to get past those barriers. Effective listening involves doing just that: finding ways to improve our own listening.

Active vs. Passive Listening

As we have discussed above, there are times when we are fully engaged in listening and times when we are doing more hearing than listening. However, even when we are consciously engaged in listening with the goal of being aware of others' communication, we still have two possibilities to choose from. We can choose to actively listen or passively listen. The difference is significant.

We will start by discussing passive listening since this is the type of listening that is most common in our day-to-day lives. Passive listening doesn't require that we pay much attention or offer much thought to the message(s) we are listening to. A great example of passive listening is how we watch and listen to television. Since we have no need to respond to TV and provide any feedback, we are not fully engaged in listening to the programs. As a result, we may often find that we can do other things, talk to other people, and focus our attention elsewhere *while* watching and listening to the TV set.

Active listening is much more engaged. When we actively listen we are we are prepared to listen, involved in the interaction, open-minded, and evaluating the message(s). As a result, we are likely to retain more information (Lewis & Reinsch, 1988).

TYPES OF LISTENING

Andrew Wolvin and Carolyn Coakley (1995) identified four distinct types of (what I have called) active listening. This categorization is useful as a way of reminding us that we can change, adapt, and adjust our listening for a variety of contexts and accomplish a variety of goals, needs, and purposes.

Listening for Appreciation

The next time you put in your earphones, turn on your personal music player and touch play on your favorite song. Ask yourself, "Why am I listening to this?" If your response is "because I like it" or "because it helps me feel something emotionally," then you are engaging in appreciative listening. When we watch television, go to a concert, attend a poetry reading, and occasionally listen to a speech, we are listening for appreciation. This means that we listen because we like what we hear, feel better, relax, get "pumped-up," or fall asleep to sounds because they are comforting and enjoyable.

Listening for Empathy

When a friend comes to you upset about a personal crisis, we find ourselves in a situation demanding we listen for empathy. When we empathize with someone, it means that we are truly able to feel and understand that person's emotions. This is perhaps one of the most important types of listening when it comes to friendships and romantic relationships, and yet causes some of the most difficult conflict. Have you ever told a friend or family member about a problem you were having hoping to get only sympathy and instead being told what you *should* do? As a parent, I am sure that I'm guilty of giving my daughter advice when what she really wanted was a sympathetic ear. There are now dozens of online courses going by all kinds of different names that teach therapists, counselors, teachers, parents, and even children how to improve their empathic listening skills.

Listening for Comprehension

As a student who has sat through many classes and prepared for many tests, you can probably relate to comprehensive listening or listening with the purpose of understanding. Having spent many years as an undergraduate and graduate student, I found myself engaging in this listening quite often. I discovered that if I was not well rested, had not eaten a balanced meal, or had not gotten my coffee intake, it was quite challenging to really focus on what the speaker was saying. I still have to do this as an instructor, listening to over 800 student speeches each year. Luckily, I truly enjoy doing this! Honestly, I appreciate as an instructor the chance to listen to students put into practice what they have been learning in class, and I have been privileged to witness some extraordinary speeches throughout my career. Although since I am grading these speeches, they also fit in the next category.

Listening Critically

Imagine that your favorite musical artist hired you next summer break to be the sound engineer for their live concerts. You were given the chance to go on tour with the band, hang out socially, and even celebrate with them. But most importantly after they trained you, you were being paid and given the responsibility to make them sound their best. Does that sound like a nice job to you? Now, imagine you had this same opportunity but with a musical artist that you do not like. In fact, you despise their music so much that you would not even accept a free download of their songs. Could you still make them sound their best? This is a real dilemma that faces sound engineers in the music industry. A sound engineer is the person responsible for combining (mixing) the disparate sounds of multiple musicians to unite them into the beautiful harmony we have come to expect from our favorite artists. They are in a sense, the most skilled, most talented, and most consummate critical listeners in the world (well, the good ones anyway). My cousin James Teitelbaum has been doing it since he was a teenager with several bands that he started and he now teaches at a top school of the arts in Chicago. The first thing he has to teach his students to do is focus on listening to the music *not* for appreciation. That is hard to do since most people who become sound engineers have a passion for music. But, what he does is have them listen to music from multiple genres and locations all over the globe with the goal of analyzing the sounds, instruments, and ways in which it all fits together.

As a critical listener, you have the obligation to try and put aside your personal opinions about the speaker and subject and recognize that you may have biases that you carry into the communication encounter. The goal of **critical listening** is to analyze, evaluate, judge, critique, and think about the message you are listening to. It demands that we pose questions about the quality and content of the messages we are receiving. We must focus on the six questions:

Who is this speaker? Are they credible in regards to this topic?

What is the purpose of this message? Is there a goal or an agenda in the speaker's message?

Why am I being given this message? Is there a particular reason that I have been chosen as the audience for the message?

Where was this information obtained? Is it valid, honest, and reliable?

When was this information collected? Is this timely, recent, and accurate?

How did this speaker obtain this information being used in the message? Do I know if the information is being embellished at all?

You can certainly expand on these questions, but that gives a very good starting point to use as a framework for exploring with a critical ear the quality and content of messages.

RESPONDING WHEN LISTENING

There is some fascinating research that has been conducted suggesting that our brains are able to think at a rate nearly 4–6 times faster than we can speak (Wolff & Marsnik, 1992). As a result, we commonly are thinking about things before someone speaking to us has even finished. And this means that it is often challenging for us to really listen to others speak.

Paraphrasing

A great way to show a speaker that you are fully listening to him/her is to use a skill called paraphrasing (Adler & Rodman, 2012). It is easy to do and yet powerful at sending the indirect message that one is listening and cares. Paraphrasing is a skill where you summarize and restate the message you have just heard someone say to you. Here's how it works: Let's say you come home and your roommate is sitting on the sofa looking upset. You ask what's wrong and you are given an earful of complaints about the dishes that have been left in the sink for too long. If you engage in paraphrasing, you might say something like, "So you are saying that you are upset and feel the dishes have been sitting in the sink for too long. Is that correct?" As you can imagine, this might very well diffuse the situation and allow the two of you to sit down, discuss the issues, and look for solutions that will make everyone happy. Now I admit not all roommate problems can be solved with communication, but sometimes better communication makes it easier to solve more problems.

Perception Checking

My former professor Ron Alder and his colleagues wrote about a method of communicating that taught two or more individuals to take paraphrasing a step further and really begin to listen to and understand each other in ways that would help them resolve conflicts (see Adler & Rodman, 2012). As an undergraduate student, we had to perform this activity while being video recorded with a classmate. I will admit it was a little awkward at first, but it really is useful.

There are three steps to the process of perception checking:

1. Describe the behavior that you see.
2. Offer at least two possible interpretations of the behavior.
3. Request clarification about how to interpret the behavior.

Here is an example: Your roommate glares at you and while putting the dishes away seems to be banging them a little bit extra than normal.

When you were quickly putting the dishes away, (description) *you seemed to be upset,* (first interpretation) *or were you just trying to get it done quickly,* (second interpretation) *how are you feeling right now?* (request clarification).

Perhaps you can see how this type of communication response is likely to seem non-defensive, non-hostile, and shows the other person that you have a sincere desire to solve a problem.

SUMMARY

Despite having little formal training in listening, in fact much less than most of us receive in speaking, it is the area of communication we spend most of our time engaged in. As a result, most of us aren't all that good at listening. However, there is hope for everyone. With some training and practice, we all can become better listeners and better communicators. If this skill improves our interpersonal relationships and helps us become better friends, partners, family members, employees, and employers, then it is a skill that will certainly improve our lives.

REFERENCES

Adler, R. B., & Rodman, G. (2012). *Understanding human communication* (11th ed.). New York, NY: Oxford.

Lewis, M. H., & Reinsch, N. L. (1988). Listening in organizational environments. *Journal of Business Communication, 25,* 49–67.

Wolff, F. I., & Marsnik, N. C. (1992). *Perceptive listening* (2nd ed.). Fort Worth, TX: Harcourt.

Wolvin, A., & Coakley, C. G. (1995). *Listening* (5th ed.). Dubuque, IA: Brown & Benchmark.

Chapter 6

Public Speaking

We are what we repeatedly do.
Excellence, then, is not an act but a habit.
—Aristotle

Key Concepts to Understand
Definition of Public Speaking
Informative Speeches
Ceremonial Speeches
Persuasive Speeches
Manuscript Delivery
Memorized Delivery
Impromptu Delivery
Extemporaneous Delivery
How to Outline Your Speech
How to Use Presentation Software
Ethics in Public Speaking

Public speaking can be thought of as a unique form of communication in that most people do not often find themselves standing behind a podium, on a stage, and speaking to an audience of hundreds or thousands of listeners. However, some people in the world of communication training and teaching argue that speaking in public is not unique at all. They say it is so ubiquitous that ALL speaking is in fact, public speaking. Certainly, there is some truth in this. Every time we speak to another person we are speaking in "public" to some degree. However, the focus of this chapter will be on the more formal definition of public speaking.

The type that most often takes place in front of an audience of twelve or more people and oftentimes while standing behind a podium or at the head of the room.

DEFINITION OF PUBLIC SPEAKING

As you may recall from Chapter 1, communication is the **exchange of messages**. So public speaking is obviously a form of communication and for the purposes of this chapter, public speaking can be thought of and defined as "an **exchange of messages <u>with</u> an audience**." Notice the definition includes the word "with" and not the word "to" an audience. It is important to remember that an effective speaker is not just talking to the audience, but is communicating with them. As we will see, communication with an audience requires much more versatility in speaking and demands the speaker be ready to change and adapt to the needs of that audience.

Public Speaking is Different from Everyday Conversations

Public speaking differs from other forms of communication in several important ways and from what you may think of as your everyday conversations (such as with friends) in five important areas.

Formal

Public speaking requires the use of more formal language than everyday conversations. Although our language choice should not be as formal as written language, it should still be more formal than the way we speak with friends. Obviously there should be less slang, less fillers, and (for some) less profanity. However, public speaking should still sound *conversational* in language choice during delivery.

Goal Directed

Effective public speaking requires that the speaker have a clear goal and purpose for presenting his or her speech. More importantly, this goal should be clearly communicated to the audience in the form of a thesis statement (more about this later). Oftentimes casual conversations are not goal-directed and in fact serve the function of maintaining our relationships by being fluid and able to change directions quickly.

Prepared

Successful speakers conduct extensive practice and preparation before delivering their speeches. Oftentimes this includes the use of video recording and utilizing demonstration audiences (this can include friends, roommates, and family members). The amount of practice needed is contingent upon the speaker's familiarity with the topic, knowledge of the audience, and experience with public speaking among other things. There is no single "right" amount of practice that can be prescribed to any individual speaker. Most of our everyday conversations are not practiced, unless we are preparing a proposal or asking for a raise. Most of us don't practice our conversations.

Role Driven

When delivering a speech, we assume the role of speaker and the audience assumes the role of listener. That does not mean they aren't giving us constant feedback, but just that they know they are expected to sit in their chairs, listen, applause when finished, and not talk during the speech. However, in our everyday conversations we are often moving fluidly between the role of speaker and listener, often assuming both roles simultaneously.

Directional

Just as we are taking on roles while delivering a speech, we are also following a formula of speaker to audience interaction that is much more one-way than our everyday conversations that are examples of much more two-way speaking. For example, in a speech we expect the speaker to do all of the talking and the audience do none (unless there is a question and answer period). In our everyday conversations, many of us would feel that if one person is doing all of the talking, they are dominating the conversation unfairly.

THE TYPES OF SPEECHES

There are three broad categories of speeches that we are likely to deliver in any public speaking class. What distinguishes these from each other is the primary goal the speaker has in delivering each of the three types.

Informative Speeches

The primary goal of informative speaking is to inform, educate, and provide the audience with new information. Some of the common types of informative speeches include: introductory speeches, how-to speeches, historical figures and events, speeches about places or things, and many more will be discussed later in the book.

Ceremonial Speeches

The primary goal of a ceremonial speech is quite different from an informative speech. First, let's think of the ceremonies where you expect to hear speeches. This includes: weddings, funerals, graduations, anniversaries, birthdays, retirements, awards and recognition events, and tributes to people, places, or things. In each of these instances, the goal is not to share information (although there may be some need to provide some background information) but instead to connect on an emotional level with your audience. These will be discussed in more detail later as well.

Persuasive Speeches

The persuasive speech is one in which the speaker has the intention of convincing the audience to change their beliefs, ideas, thoughts, feelings, and/or actions. Although many informative speeches can lead audience members to change as a result of the information they hear, an effective persuasive speech takes the process one step further by calling the audience to take some sort of action (the "call to action"). This will also be discussed in much more detail later in the book.

The Three Areas of Effective Speeches

There are three important criteria in creating successful speeches of any type. As an audience member, these three criteria serve as a useful tool for measuring the quality and effectiveness of any speech.

Content

The first area to keep in mind relates to the content of the speech. Content is the information that goes into the speech. This includes the topic and how relevant it is to the audience, how well the ideas are supported, and how clear and direct the language was for the audience.

Organization

Second is how well the speech was organized and easy to follow. All speeches have at the minimum three major sections: The introduction, the body, and the conclusion. For the purpose of effectiveness, I often suggest that speakers divide the introduction into two parts, separating the introduction from the thesis. Each of the sections is organized to meet a specific need. When the organization is effective, the speech is easy to follow, flows between points, and main points are easy to identify.

Introduction. A great introduction meets two primary goals: To grab the audience's attention and to preview the speech. There are five ways to begin your speech; however, only one is highly recommended. Speakers can begin with (1) a joke, although there is always the risk that it misses the mark or isn't as funny as was expected. You could begin with (2) a quote, but there is the chance that the audience may find themselves confused about when the quote begins or ends, or may begin thinking about the quote's author (a good speaker cites his or her sources) and not listening to the speech. One could also begin with (3) some statistics, data, charts, graphs, or visuals, but the risk with those is that many audience members may find too match data overwhelming, or even boring. These are usually better off saved for later in the speech. Another option that many consider is the use of (4) asking a question. Be careful of asking the audience a rhetorical question (one you only want them to think about) because someone may blurt out and answer. Also be careful of asking a question that you need them to answer, as they may not respond. The best way to begin a speech is to (5) tell a story. The benefits of a story are that when done well, the audience can connect with the speaker on an emotional level. A good story puts the audience right into the action. Think of the best books you have read. They don't say "imagine," they just begin with the opening of the story. Use powerful, descriptive, and vivid language that paints a detailed picture in your audience's minds-eye.

Body. The body of the speech includes your main points. I suggest to most speakers that they limit the number of main points to between two and five if possible. It might be easy for your audience to remember the main points if they can count them on one hand. In addition to the main points, effective speeches utilize transitions between main points. Transitions are simply brief sentences that allow the audience to easily follow along. These can be alpha-numeric (such as saying "first" or "A") or they can be contextual such as saying, "Not only was he hard-working, but he was also successful." (For a description of the details within your main points, see below.)

Conclusion. The goal of an effective conclusion is twofold. It should summarize the message and leave the audience with something memorable as well. Just as was discussed in the section on your introduction, you could also use jokes, quotes, statistics, rhetorical questions, and (ideally) stories.

Types of Organizational Structures

Carefully considering how to organize your speech will help you to better connect with the audience and make the speech easier to follow, more memorable, and more effective. There are three primary ways you can organize your main points.

Chronological
Following the chronological organizational structure means that your main points follow a sequential time-line. This is a great way to organize a speech that informs the audience how to do something or that provides some historical background of a person, place, or location.

Spatial
Following the spatial organizational structure means that your main points follow the organization structure of using physical space. This is ideal for a speech that could coordinate with a map (such as the largest national forests from northern to southern California) or that describes a location (such as an informative speech on the museum of natural history) or even an informative speech about the sports injuries one has received (from head to toe).

Topical
The final organizational structure is the catchall, everything else category. Following the topical structure can be almost anything not covered above. For example, the three ways I chose my major, three things I learned from my study abroad, or three characteristics about my grandfather that make him worthy of praise.

DELIVERY

When most of us think about a great speech, our first thought probably goes directly to delivery. However, all three of the elements of effective speeches are equally important. There is no single "right" way to deliver a speech. While many experts claim that certain types of posture or numerous hand gestures are needed, when these are incorporated into a speech in an unnatural way, most of us would feel that the speaker seems awkward, uncomfortable, and artificial. So, in reality, the ideal delivery style makes the speaker look comfortable, confident, and authentic.

However, of the four delivery styles for most presentations, only one will usually make the speaker look natural.

Manuscript

Delivery by use of reading a manuscript (although common in many political arenas) is less than ideal. Most audiences find a speaker that is reading his or her notes to them to be less effective. There are certainly exceptions to this (Steve Jobs delivered an excellent graduation speech at Stanford University that was almost entirely read from the podium). Many politicians and historical figures have delivered speeches by manuscript to great acclaim (John F. Kennedy and Martin Luther King, Jr. come to mind). However, if you are delivering a business presentation, reading your notes may seem like you are unprepared, lack confidence, and potentially lack credibility.

Memorized

It is not advisable to attempt to memorize your speech. When you get nervous, you could easily forget what you wanted to say in the middle of your speech. And unlike most actors on a stage who have another actor or director behind the curtain to call out lines, speakers are usually on their own behind the podium. Even with some skill in memorization, trying to recite your speech by memory defeats the purpose of communication *with* an audience. If you needed to change, adjust, or adapt, you would not be able to do so.

Impromptu

This delivery style is a great skill to have, and many public speaking classes will require you to give an impromptu speech. This is when you just have to stand up and speak. You don't have the option or time to practice, so you would not have been able to do more than jot down a few notes very quickly. If you have been invited (or hired) to deliver a speech to an audience at a specific time and place, it would be unwise to deliver the speech with the impromptu method (meaning you have not practiced or prepared). That in simple English is called "winging it."

Extemporaneous

The ideal delivery style is known as extemporaneous. It is practiced and prepared, but never read or memorized completely. The speaker can read important quotes and data/statistics. She can also memorize the introduction and stories that are part of the speech. However, she is essentially having a conversation with the audience and is able to change, modify, and adapt to necessary variations in the time, venue, and audience needs. This delivery style sounds the most prepared and with effective practice will make the speaker sound the most confident, knowledgeable, and well groomed.

OUTLINING SPEECHES

Speeches should be organized along the basic outline format rather than written out as an essay. It is a great way to save time and still quickly and easily organize the speech so that it is prepared for delivery and most importantly, to aid you in delivering the speech extemporaneously.

Outline Styles

Many experts suggest that the speaker develop two outlines in the preparation of the speech. The first is often referred to as the Formal Outline or sometimes the Preparation Outline. This outline is usually written out in detail and with complete sentences. However, in reality, many students (in an effort to save time) may want to skip this step and begin with the second outline style known as the Informal Outline or the Speaking Outline.

Sample Informal Speaking Outline Format

   I. Introduction
  II. Thesis
 III. Body
     Transition
    A. Main Point
      1. Sub-point
        a) Sub sub-point
        b) Sub sub-point
    Transition

    B. Main Point
       1. Sub-point
          a) Sub sub-point
          b) Sub sub-point
    Transition
IV. Conclusion
V. References

We have already discussed the purpose of the introduction, main points, and conclusion. Now let's look at the details.

Thesis

The thesis is a single sentence that serves to preview the purpose and goal of the speech in a way that helps the listener identify the main points. So the thesis should let us know what the main points would be. For example, a great thesis sentence for a speech about my love of photography might sound like this:

> *My love of photography has helped open my eyes to different cultures, become my creative outlet, and helped me to choose a journalism major.*

Just by hearing this thesis sentence, you can easily determine the three main points of the speech. This will make it simple and easy to follow for the listener.

Main Points
(See above)

Sub-points
After you have given us the main points, it is most effective if the speaker briefly explains that main point. For example, if my first main point were "hard work," it would make sense to then define and explain what it means to me. Clearly "hard work" means different things to different people. For example, if my first main point was that my grandfather was a hardworking man, I should then explain how he was a hardworking man. I could say "my grandfather was so hardworking that he was up every day at 6 a.m. to feed the cows on our farm, even if it was raining, snowing, or Christmas morning."

Sub Sub-points

The purpose of the sub sub-points is simply to explain and illustrate the main points. Generally, the ideal form of explanation is to tell stories and/or use quotes. In an ideal speech, there would be two examples/illustrations because that would make the support stand out much stronger.

Transitions

(See above)

The basic format of the speech outline does not have to be grammatically correct nor does it have to meet the requirements of an effective English paper. The outline is YOUR copy of notes and should be made as easy to use and as effective as possible to give you the information you need to communicate with the audience, and avoid reading a manuscript or trying to memorize the speech.

How to Use Presentation Software Effectively
Contributed by Diane Auten

Gone are the days when we could give a presentation and simply bring along a poster board with cutouts from magazines and drawings of our own. Modern audiences expect more technology and demand something that looks highly professional. Microsoft answered this call by developing the program PowerPoint as part of the suite of Office software. Apple computers developed Keynote that is quite similar to PowerPoint. And recently a Hungarian company developed "Prezi," an online, cloud-based presentation program (meaning you don't have to buy and install the program, you can use it online).

Unfortunately, as a quick Internet search will support, far too many speakers use presentation technology in ways that are ineffective and detract from the success of the speech. With new technology comes a need to use it differently than we used old technology. Most audiences will be highly disappointed if the focus of the presentation is on the screen and not the speaker. An audience should not feel that they need to give more of their attention to the screen than the speaker.

Remember that the PowerPoint presentation should not **be** your presentation, but it should complement what you are saying. It should never be able to stand alone. People often ask me to email my PowerPoint when they miss one of my lectures or a presentation that I am giving. I always tell them that the PowerPoint will mean nothing without the presentation. And that's how it should be.

In the book *Presentation Zen*, author Garr Reynolds (2011) talks about something called the split attention effect. This theory focuses on the problems we encounter when we have too much text on Power-Point. Firstly, it's important to know that our brain processes information through two different channels: The visual channel (sight) and the verbal channel (language). The split attention effect occurs when competing messages are sent in the verbal channel. This results in our brains having to split our attention between two different competing stimuli. Let me give you an example. Let's say that you are sitting and reading a really good book and you are engrossed in the content of the book (verbal). Then your friend comes up to you while you are reading and starts to tell you a really awesome story about their weekend (another verbal message). You love your book too much to put it down, so you are reading your book and listening to your friend at the same time. That is an example of two competing messages in the verbal channel. It's impossible for you to read the book and get the complete understanding of the content, while also listening to your friend tell their juicy story (and get the complete message from the story). Your brain can really only handle one of those things at a time if it's going to fully get the message. What will happen is you pick up bits and pieces of the book while tuning out your friend, or you pick up bits and pieces of the story your friend is telling while still reading your book. (How many times have you read a page in a textbook, gotten to the bottom of the page, and said, "I have no idea what I just read"? That is the split attention effect in full swing).

So when you put words in paragraph form up on the screen (processed through the verbal channel because it is language) and then you talk (verbal message) while the audience is reading, the audience is forced to split their attention between these dual and competing messages. If they are also trying to take notes while you speak (a third verbal message), it will be impossible for them to comprehend the entire presentation. This is problematic because it is often frustrating and can even be stressful for the audience.

So what is the solution? Here are my suggestions:

- Use slides for images more often than text.
- When using text, keep it to short bullet points NOT long sentences.
- Make sure the font is large enough to be seen from the back of the room.
- Use limited colors and graphics so that the slides don't become too busy and distracting.
- Avoid too many sound bites, transition effects, and moving objects.

(continued)

How to Use Presentation Software Effectively (continued)

Also remember the audience does not want to look at the same slide for 15 minutes. In our short attention span world, this causes a lot of problems and bores an audience. Did you know that in Microsoft PowerPoint if you hit the letter "B" on your keyboard your screen will go black, and if you hit the letter "W" it will go white? If you don't want the audience to focus on the screen, but instead to focus on you, try using those tricks.

So, the goal is to pick simple pictures that represent what you are talking about. Sometimes you don't need any language on the slides at all, especially if the audience is not taking notes. Often when I am presenting to an audience and they are just there for enjoyment, I don't have words at all on my slides. However, if I want my audience to understand that we have switched to a new main point or that the topic has changed, I will put a clear simple heading on each slide so they understand.

Hopefully you have a better idea of what your PowerPoint should look like: clean, simple slides. Let YOU, the speaker, be the center of attention and the focus of the presentation, not your PowerPoint.

ETHICS IN PUBLIC SPEAKING

It would be impossible to have a textbook on public speaking without having a discussion on ethics. However, the way in which one defines ethics is likely as varied as the number of people reading this book. So in reality it is difficult, if not impossible to define what it means to be an ethical speaker. However, it is still valuable to attempt the exercise and at least try to find some mutually agreed upon qualities that most would consider define an ethical speaker. So, examine these scenarios and ask yourself if the speaker was unethical:

> *A speaker at a high school calls special needs students "retarded" and makes fun of them.*

> *A male politician insults his female opponent by making a joke about her breasts.*

> *A religious speaker says that members of other religions don't deserve to go to heaven.*

How would you feel if you heard any of the above? Are any of those unethical in your opinion?

Following is a list of things that many communication instructors feel helps to define ethical speaking, myself included. Do you agree or disagree with these?

Speakers should:

- Be truthful, accurate, and honest.
- Allow free expression and should not constrain the free expression of ideas.
- Support diversity of opinion and allow and accept others to express diverse opinions.
- Show respect to the audience members.
- Strive for mutual understanding of other communicators.
- Create climates of caring and supportive speaking opportunities.
- Commit to allowing expression of personal convictions and beliefs.
- Advocate sharing of opinions, information, and ideas while still respecting privacy and confidentiality.
- Provide an environment that never degrades, condemns, distorts, coerces, is intolerant of others, or promotes hatred of people.
- Accept responsibility for their words, actions, tone, body language, and consequences of speech.

Adapted from O'Hair, Steward, and Rubenstein (2009).

SUMMARY

The most important part of a speech is the preparation that goes into getting it ready for delivery. And at the top of that list is the organization of the speech as evidenced by the outline that the speaker prepares in advance.

REFERENCES

O'Hair, D., Stewart, R., & Rubenstein, H. (2009). *A speaker's guidebook.* Bedford/St. Martin's.

Reynolds, G. (2011). *Presentation Zen: Simple ideas on presentation design and delivery* (2nd ed.). Berkeley, CA: New Riders.

Chapter 7

Overcoming Nerves

The only thing we have to fear is fear itself.
—Franklin D. Roosevelt

Key Concepts to Understand
Communication Apprehension
Visualization
Systematic Desensitization
Cognitive Restructuring

Upon telling people I meet that I am a speech communication teacher and consultant, I'm usually told that public speaking was the class they dreaded the most in college (nice opening line huh?). There were several surveys conducted in the late 1970s (that have been misquoted ever since) claiming that we would rather die than give a presentation. During my nearly 15 years teaching communication, I personally have met many people who feel very uncomfortable speaking in front of groups, but honestly I have yet to meet anyone who would rather be dead than give a speech. I think if I had a pitchfork to your backside, you would give the speech.

However, the question I am most often asked is: How do I overcome my fear of speaking? The answer is both simple and complex. The short answer is: speak. That's right, the more you do it, the more comfortable you will feel. But in reality, most people don't have a great deal of opportunity to speak in front of different groups on a regular basis. So let me give you the more complex answer. There are a few simple tricks that you can use to help you feel more comfortable speaking in front of groups. First and foremost is: practice, practice, practice.

COMMUNICATION APPREHENSION

My own personal surveys suggest that between 70 to 90 percent of my students admit to getting nervous when giving speeches. I personally have found that in certain situations, I too can get nervous. Several years ago I was invited to give a presentation at U.C. Santa Barbara, my Alma matter. Knowing that I had to speak well and present myself effectively in front of all of my old professors (despite that I was no longer their student and no longer being graded) made me nervous. As a result, I spoke too quickly and felt my talk was less than ideal.

So where does the fear of speaking come from? Scientists and speech experts seem to have several different theories. Perhaps the most common and most supported with credible research is that of James McCroskey who passed away in December of 2012 and Virginia Richmond. They found that a number of people seemed to possess a fear of not only speaking in public, but in fact, communication with others in general. According to these researchers, communication apprehension (or CA for short) is an individual's fear associated with a real (or anticipated) communication event with another person. CA is a psychological response to being judged and evaluated by others. This becomes a physical response as our bodies perceive the threat of speaking as a danger to our physical well-being. The result is that we engage our circulatory and adrenal systems to prepare us for the "fight or flight" response. Since we (usually) don't run from the communication situation, our bodies responds with an increase heart rate, sweating, and other normal fear responses. The challenge for most speakers lies in the normal and natural response of our bodies to these fearful and stressful situations.

Although there is still a debate today about the origins of the fear of public speaking and potential cures, it seems evident that it is (a) quite common and (b) can be reduced with certain tactics that will be explained in the remainder of this chapter (Richmond & McCroskey, 1992).

Videotape Yourself Practicing

There is something you can do when you do practice that will dramatically improve your speaking and at the same time help you feel more prepared, more practiced, and less nervous. Research shows that when speakers practice by videotaping themselves and reviewing the videotapes, they see a 10 to 20 percent increase in their effectiveness in front of an audience. This is more effective when you practice in front of the camera two or more times for each speech.

Professional debaters, lawyers, and those undergoing serious speech coaching are videotaped often during practice sessions. What if you don't have access to a video camera? Although in this day and age, most people do have the ability to record video on smart phones, laptops, and tablets, at the very least, record your voice using a digital recorder, old-fashioned tape player, or personal computer with a microphone. This allows you to hear what you sound like to an audience. The drawback is that you can't see your nonverbal communication—oftentimes the most important part of the presentation. I do not recommend that you ask a significant other to view your presentation and give feedback. It's been my experience that too many "suggestions" can start arguments . . . or worse.

Next, before you talk, relax, breath, and smile! Smiling makes your brain feel good and your body less nervous. If you don't know people in the audience, try to arrive early and introduce yourself to a few people. It always helps to have some (new) familiar, smiling faces out there.

Visualization

For those of you who still have some fears about speaking, there are three excellent strategies that are used to help people in your situation. The first strategy is one that is used by virtually all professional athletes and has become more popular in collegiate athletics and even high school sports. It's called *visualization*. And, it works. Here's what you do. (1) Find a quiet place to sit or stand without any interruptions for at least 10 to 20 minutes. (2) Mentally "walk" yourself through the presentation at the beginning, seeing yourself being introduced, seeing the smiles and excitement on the faces of the people in the audience. As you walk to the podium, feel how confident and ready you feel for the presentation. Continue walking yourself through the entire presentation, allowing yourself the possibility of a simple mistake . . . one that goes fine and that you recover from so smoothly that the audience doesn't even notice. Don't expect yourself to be more than human. (3) Complete your visualization by seeing yourself succeed and giving an outstanding presentation. Notice how pleased the audience is with what you've said. Repeat this several times for a couple of days before your big speech. You'll find that you are less nervous and feel more confident.

Systematic Desensitization

The second method that is often used to help people overcome presentation anxiety is called: **Systematic Desensitization (SD)**. Developed in the early 1950s as a form of treatment for many different types of fears, since the early 1970s it has been used more extensively for stage fright (or what researchers term communication apprehension), and when used in training programs, it works well. Here's how:

All humans have a natural response to any situation that we consider threatening. Our normal response is fight or flight. But, if we can't run, our bodies naturally prepare for the "fight" response. This includes becoming tense and the tightening of our muscles . . . an all too common response to stressful situations for many of us!

SD is based on the belief that when a response other than tension and stress (such as muscle relaxation) is to be applied, individuals will learn to better manage and cope with a particularly stressful situation.

So, the basic premise is: RELAX! Sounds easy . . . but it's hard to do when you have a presentation to give. The reality is this: we have to **learn** to use SD. In programs people are taught how to relax their muscles by first tensing them and then releasing while using breathing and relaxation techniques. With practice, this can be done on command.

The next step is to introduce the participant to the stressful situation. First gradually (such as imagine talking with a stranger) and then progressively working toward the most stressful situations (imagine the speech) within a few hours. By the time this occurs, participants have learned and practiced associating relaxation, not tension with these stressful situations. The process is very effective and affordable. A handful of 1-hour sessions leads to dramatic results.

Cognitive Restructuring

While SD focuses on muscle tension or the body's response to stress, another technique focuses on the brain's response to stress called: **Cognitive Restructuring (CR)**. CR teaches us to rethink how we label and evaluate certain situations. Deep down we know that if we make a mistake on this upcoming presentation it won't be the end of the world . . . yet sometimes we act like it will! CR is a process of changing our belief systems, by exposing how irrational some of our beliefs really are (e.g., I must be perfect, Everyone must like me, etc.).

This is accomplished in four steps. First, we must identify the negative self-statements that we often make about any situation. Second, each of these statements must be analyzed and exposed for errors in logic. These statements can ultimately <u>cause</u> us to do poorly (self-fulfilling prophecies). Third, we learn a new set of coping statements to say to ourselves. These are not just positive affirmations, but realistic statements. Fourth, we practice these statements. We must recognize that given how many years we have been repeating the negative statements, we can't expect perfection right away. But with time and crucial practice (insight alone is not enough), we can replace the negative with positive statements. Keep in mind that the focus is on learning the new statements, not analyzing the reasons for the negative (that could take years of therapy). CR has been highly effective at helping people overcome presentation anxiety and with the right trainer should work well for you.

The final strategy for improving your presentation is **skills training**. Take a public speaking class (I assume you are, and that's why you have this textbook), a presentation skills workshop, or undergo coaching (your speech instructor may be able to help with coaching). After all, Martin Luther King, Jr. and John F. Kennedy both had help with their speeches . . . and look how well it worked for them!

SUMMARY

Lastly remember this: Most people get nervous giving speeches and you can't tell just by looking at them, so you are not alone. Practice as much as you can, and allow yourself to feel some of the nerves. It's natural for humans to thrive on adrenaline rushes (look at how many people parachute, bungee jump, hang glide, and ride skateboards). A little bit of an adrenaline rush will help you feel excited, and when used to your advantage help you look and sound more animated and enthusiastic about your topic.

REFERENCES

Franklin D. Roosevelt inaugural address, March 4, 1933 from
www.pbs.org

Richmond, V. P., & McCroskey, J. C. (1992). *Communication: Apprehension, avoidance, and effectiveness* (3rd ed.). Scottsdale, AZ: Gorsuch Scarisbrick.

Chapter 8

Understanding and Analyzing Your Audience

The only good is knowledge and the only evil is ignorance.
—Socrates

Key Concepts to Understand
Definition of Audience
Demographics
Psychographics
Audience Research Methods

The most important component of every single speech you will ever give is always the audience. There has never been, nor will there ever be a great (or even a good) speech that was NOT delivered to an audience. Therefore, understanding the audience is the most critical step an effective speaker can take prior to working on the speech itself.

AUDIENCE ANALYSIS

Effective speaking requires taking time to clearly understand whom your audience is, and what drives, motivates, inspires, and even upsets this group of people. Focus on the attitudes, beliefs, and opinions of your listeners. If you are effectively able to gauge these dynamics, you will be able to adapt to and connect with more people than by speaking unprepared.

Adapting to your audience will help you connect with the listeners in four important ways:

Positive First Impressions

As the old cliché goes, we never get a second chance to make a first impression. This is certainly applicable to public speaking. As a speaker who shows knowledge of the audience, you immediately give the impression that you care about them and are there to meet their needs, not your own.

Why Should They Listen to You?

When they know you are there to meet their own needs, they are more likely to listen to you and be open to receiving your message. After all, every audience member comes to a speech with preconceived notions about others. These can be projected onto a speaker in the form of stereotypes and judgments based on the visual cues made about the speaker (gender, age, clothing, etc.).

Credibility and Likeability

After the audience has decided they are willing to listen to you, they will continue to judge you as a speaker in terms of credibility and likeability. Chances are, if they feel that you have their best interest at heart, understand them as both an audience and as individuals, and respect them, they will be more likely to consider you a credible speaker (more on this topic later in the book).

Speak Appropriately and Avoid Offending the Audience

Finally, with effective research you will be able to make judgments about what expectations your audience will have in listening to you speak. It will be much easier to predict if you can use particular types of humor, certain language such as slang terms, and references to concepts that may be known only to some members of society. In turn, this should reduce the risk of being offensive or inappropriate during your speech.

Two Characteristics of Audience Analysis

A public speaking audience can be defined as:

A collection of people receiving messages from a speaker.

However, this broad definition doesn't take into account the unique characteristics of each audience and the myriad ways that these individuals have unique goals and purposes for listening to a speech. Additionally, audiences can have many similar characteristics that will help the speaker to better connect with them. In an ideal world, we would like to personally know (or meet) each and every member of the audience and understand what motivates their decision to be there, what they would like to hear about, and what they already think about our topic. In reality, that is usually impossible to do before a speech. As a result, we often have to make some generalizations about our audience based on things that we can find out without meeting each and every person beforehand.

Demographics

These are characteristics about our audience that we can use to generalize, summarize, and categorize people into similar groups or subgroups. Knowing these characteristics help us tailor and target our message to these specific people. For example, if you know that your audience is entirely college students (and probably an instructor as well), it might make sense to talk about text messaging, tweeting, and social media. Yet, if you know your audience is the age of most grandparents, you may be concerned that many people will not be as familiar with those technologies.

We obviously will never know everything about an audience and are often limited to our assumptions about these demographics. The major challenge for effective speakers is to recognize that assumptions about demographics often borderline on stereotypes that can lead us to be less effective as speakers. For example, my 90-year-old grandmother was quite effective at using computers, email, and early social media. She was deeply involved in chat rooms (when they were quite popular among Internet users in the late 1990s) and really enjoyed chatting with strangers online. It would be a stereotype to suggest that all

senior citizens are unable to use new technologies and would not understand a speech on these hi-tech topics.

Age

We can look at the age of our audience in several ways. You can determine an age range, an average age, or several categories of ages (such
as 20–30; 30–40; 40–50, etc.). Each of these has some advantages and
disadvantages. If the age range is narrow (say 18–23), it may be easier to
target a message than if that range is broad (such as 19–47). Having an
average age could make it easier to estimate what memories audience
members have of historical events (if the average age is 19, most audience members were quite young on September 11, 2001). If you have
categorized audience members into groupings of ages that encompass
a broad range and multiple categories, it may be difficult to assess the
commonalities of their experiences and connections to specific historical contexts. In any case, knowing something about the age ranges of
your audience gives you an advantage in preparing your speech and
connecting with the listeners.

Gender or Sex

While it is quite useful to know if you have more men than women in the
audience, be careful not to stereotype your audience with the use of re-
marks that may be perceived as sexist. For example, assuming that men
know how to change a spare tire and women do not would most likely be
a stereotype and could be offensive to some members of the audience.
Although some topics may be of more interest to one gender over another, any topic can be adapted to your audience. A recent informative
speech delivered in one of my public speaking courses on "what to expect as you go through the trimesters (stages) of pregnancy" was clearly
tailored for women in the room. However, the speaker made sure to remind men that this information would help them to support, be more involved with, and better understand what their partners would be going
through, should they find themselves in that situation down the road.

Ethnicity

This is the classification of audience members along cultural characteristics that relate to origin, family background, (sometimes) nationality,
language, shared customs, history, etc. As with gender, be careful not to

stereotype about your audience. The challenge with checking boxes that identify our ethnicity is that we often feel that our own unique experiences lead us to have diverse attitudes, interests, and opinions on topics that others who check the same boxes on surveys will hold. One of my favorite comedians George Lopez (look him up on YouTube) often makes references to words (in Spanish), cultural symbols, foods, and such that I do not understand at all. I still find him funny, but sadly, I occasionally feel left out when the audience is laughing hysterically for reasons I just don't understand.

Education

Your audience's education levels will help you choose specific subjects and topics and direct how you approach those in a manner that they will be able to connect with. In some communication classes, you may want to subcategorize this into specific majors, years in college, and the completion of certain courses. For example, if you are going to share some statistics in a speech, you want to know that your audience has completed an introductory statistics class. If you want to talk about economics, it is helpful to know what classes your audience has completed. Again, remember not to stereotype your audience. After all, both Bill Gates and Steve Jobs did not graduate from college, but they seem like very intelligent people.

Socio-Economic Status (Income, Occupation)

Another common variable used in analyzing audiences looks at income and occupation (these can be measured together or separately). While this information can clearly tell us about our audience in terms of spending ability and what we expect them to be able to afford, it is another variable that can lead to stereotypes and over-generalizations. It would be incorrect to assume that everyone making over a million dollars a year would be opposed to increased taxes or someone making under $20,000 is in favor of increasing the minimum wage. However, it does give the speaker a better picture of what the audience earns and that may be valuable if your goal is to persuade them on financial topics, tax issues, etc.

Others

Depending on your topic, you may want to know more about other demographics such as the political parties they affiliate with, the religions they identify with, their marital status, if they have children, and even the types of pets they have, the cars they drive, the clothing they wear, the location they live, and perhaps many more. It is up to the speaker to determine what information will be useful in tailoring and targeting your message to your audience.

PSYCHOGRAPHICS

Measuring demographics only gives us part of the picture of what our audience truly thinks about and cares about. Advertisers are acutely aware of this and have come up with another way to measure our audience using much more complex variables that go beyond simply determining the outer characteristics. These are referred to as psychographics (as in psychological and graphics). These variables that examine the psychological complexities of the audience allow speakers to better understand the motivations and feelings our audience members have about particular topics. For example, while most men would check the box that says MALE for gender (some people who consider themselves transgendered may choose not to place themselves in that category), it is difficult to make assumptions about gender roles, housework, marriage, etc. just by knowing the percentage of your audience who are male. Measuring the psychographics of the men in your audience would give you better information. There are three categories of psychographics that can be measured.

Attitudes

Attitudes can be thought of as our likes and dislikes. They are shaped and influenced by our values and beliefs and in turn affect our behaviors. Examples of attitudes include: taste in music, clothing, movies, television, and books (to name a few). As a speaker, you have a real advantage if you know the attitudes your audience has towards your speech topic. It will allow you to customize your message in a way to coincide with those attitudes, and when asking your audience to change will guide you in limiting how much you can expect them to change.

Values

Values are judgments that we make about what is good/bad, fair/unfair, honest/dishonest, just/unjust, moral/immoral, and virtuous/evil. Values can be measured with common words that describe things we all hold near and dear to our hearts. For example, "freedom" is something most of us value (on a national level, but also within our own day-to-day lives). Another example of a value is "justice." While this can clearly mean different things to different people, chances are few audience members would be *against* justice.

Our values guide our actions; however, we may often be inconsistent in behaving in ways that match our values. Countless examples of political and religious leaders preaching morality but failing to practice what they preach can be found with a quick Google search (look up the Reverend Jimmy Swaggart).

Beliefs

Our beliefs are often deeply held opinions about what we consider to be true. Our faith would clearly fit into this category, but so would many of our political opinions as well. Some of our beliefs are commonly shared with people in our own demographics, and others are quite unique and can even seem controversial when shared. In a college classroom, it is likely that people will have many beliefs in common and at the same time many other beliefs that cover a broad spectrum of topics and opinions. I personally have a belief that the website Wikipedia is not a credible, accurate, and useful tool for conducting research on a speech topic. While I accept that many students do not share this belief (although many other college instructors agree with me), it is a belief that I cling to dearly and therefore my students should NOT use that particular website in lieu of a more credible research source (more on this later).

Behaviors

The actions we take when it comes to voting, purchasing, watching TV, reading, and our day-to-day activities fit into the category of behaviors. Advertisers are most concerned with our spending behaviors (and changing those to purchase their specific products). Behaviors differ from attitudes, values, and beliefs in that we can observe other's behaviors and measure them in action. Let's look at all four of these psychographics together. I feel that donating organs is important (attitude) because I respect human life (value) and because having enough organs available for the large waiting list is necessary to save lives (belief), so I have signed the organ donor card on my driver's license (behavior).

Measuring Audience Demographics and Psychographics

The first decision I need to make before analyzing my audience is to choose a sample (some of the members) or measure everyone. If my speech is to a small public speaking class, it may be easy to measure everyone. If my speech is taking place at a business meeting with a large audience far away, it may be impossible to measure them all. In an ideal world, if I do select only a sample, I would like to select a **representative sample**. This is only possible if I can randomly choose people to measure and if I have access to a list of ALL audience members. Sometimes the best I can hope for is a **convenience sample** of audience members, meaning I measure some of the audience members whom I have easy access to connect with.

There are three primary ways to measure my audience and my choice in which to use depends greatly on the information that I want to acquire, the number of people I can measure, and the time I have to make sense of my findings.

If I have a large audience and will be measuring a large group of audience members or the entire audience, a **survey** may be the best way to go. Surveys utilize questions and when written and collected efficiently can be very quick and easy ways to get simple or detailed information from the audience. I can ask them to answer **open ended** or **closed ended** questions depending on the level of detail needed. Closed questions give them a choice of answers such as yes or no or check the box that represents your age.

They can also be used to measure a range of answers such as "Circle the number between 1 and 5 where 1 is Strongly Disagree and 5 is Strongly Agree." For example:

Strongly Disagree	Somewhat Disagree	No Opinion	Somewhat Agree	Strongly Agree
1	2	3	4	5

These types of questions are only as useful as the analysis done afterwards and can often require statistical measurements to make adequate sense of them. Open ended questions give your respondents more freedom in choosing their answers, yet still allow you to get detailed information. For example, you can ask people to write their age (instead of checking a box of age-ranges) or you can ask them to write their gender (instead of checking male or female). Sometimes you may want to include both types of questions on your survey. Many surveys will begin with closed questions, or forced choice questions (as they are often called), and will follow up with open ended questions such as "please explain" and some blank space for people to write in more details.

Sometimes you want only detailed answers and will choose to use questionnaires instead of surveys. Although they are quite similar (and sometimes used interchangeably), the primary difference is that **questionnaires** *are open-ended written responses that let your respondent provide as much detail as he or she desires.* The benefit of this measurement device is the greater detail and occasionally unexpected results that you may get. The downside is that they demand more complex analysis to make sense of your findings and can be quite time-consuming when collected from a large group of people.

The third type of measurement device is the use of **interviews**. These are opportunities to speak directly with members of your audience. They can be conducted in person or through the use of technology (such as with phone calls or video conferences). The primary benefit of interviews is your ability to get detailed information directly from audience members in their own words. However, the researcher must be careful not to guide or direct the respondent into answering the questions in any way. Another risk with interviews may be that respondents feel they are not being conducted anonymously and therefore may choose not to answer with complete honesty. I was once hired to speak to a large organization on the topic of effective communication. The management felt that the employees were not communicating effectively and would benefit from some skills training in how to be more effective. Prior to my presentation, I spoke with several employees about their communication in the workplace. Despite what management had told me (and hired me to work on), all of the employees I spoke with claimed there were no communication problems and everything was perfect. I later found out that the employees I spoke with were fearful that management would single them out as poor employees if they admitted they had any communication problems and thus gave me the answers they felt were in their best interest, even though they were not accurate.

While there are numerous books addressing the topic of informational interviews, I will briefly highlight five things a speaker can do to collect good, useful, and accurate information.

1. Come prepared to the interview with questions written in advance and an effective way to record answers (always ask upfront if you can digitally record the interview).

2. Build rapport with the interviewee by sharing the purpose of the interview and how the information will be used. Tell them a little about yourself and know about the interviewee in advance.

3. Conduct the interview professionally. Obviously, dressing appropriately is important, as is starting and ending on time. Good nonverbal communication, eye contact, and body language are all important. However, what will really make you look and sound professional is the preparation that you do in advance. Know about the interviewee, know about his or her organization, know about the industry in which they are employed, and ask questions that illustrate your knowledge and preparation.

4. Review your notes as soon as possible after the interview. Ask your interviewee if you can follow up if you have any additional questions and use this to clarify anything that is not clear.

5. Ask for permission before using the information in your presentation. While an employee in your audience may have provided you excellent information, using their name during your speech (without asking first) could be upsetting or even humiliating to that person. Although many audiences would appreciate you making reference to people in the room whom they all know, doing so without permission could create ill will and damage your credibility.

Other Audience Analysis

In addition to knowing something about the particular audience members, it may be useful to analyze the specific speaking situation as well. The two primary types of audiences can greatly influence their attention and focus on your speech. When we choose to go and listen to a speech, we are a **voluntary** audience. However, when we are forced to hear a speech for school or work that is required, we are considered a **captive** audience.

Size of the Audience

When speaking to a large audience, you may be equipped with a microphone and may even have a video camera recording you and projecting the video live on screen. Although these types of speeches are not common for most of us, they certainly will merit some preparation.

Most of us will be speaking in small groups or small rooms without amplification, but often with visual technology such as a computer and projector. Chances are there will be some interruptions, comments or questions, and very little space between the speaker and audience. Language may need to be far more conversational than in large formal speaking situations and your voice may need to be monitored carefully to project to all ends of the room without sounding like you are screaming at them. It can certainly have some unique challenges. Knowing about these challenges in advance will save you time, stress, and last minute accommodation challenges.

Occasion

The reason for the event at which you are speaking is important to think about before preparing your speech. Ask the question: Why are we here? Is this a business meeting that demands an informative talk or one better suited to some humor and fun? Sometimes the speaker may want to incorporate some of the occasion into his or her speech. This could include the history of the event and/or occasion.

Environment

Some speeches take place indoors in meeting facilities while others can occur outdoors at graduation ceremonies, in open-air amphitheaters, or even sports arenas. Speaking outdoors can be quite a challenge because of nearby traffic noise, large audiences, or sometimes airplanes flying overhead. Not to mention the sun, heat, or sometimes rain that occurs when under the elements.

I was recently at a conference where Stedman Graham (better known to some as Oprah's man) was a keynote speaker. The purpose of the meeting was for professionals in the speaking fields to share ideas and collaborate with each other. The talk given by the speaker was geared towards an audience of speakers. He spoke about how he got started as a speaker, and what he did in the industry. His nonverbal communication was geared well toward the specific location. He walked around the room and got close to people. He made direct eye contact with people sitting near the aisles. He used his voice to control the intensity with which we listened, getting quiet when it was serious and louder when it was humorous. He did an excellent job of understanding his audience and the speaking situation as a whole.

SUMMARY

The more a speaker knows about her audience, the better she will be able to adapt to the audience and connect with them. The speech should be more informative, more persuasive, and more interesting to the audience when it is tailored directly to them. However, at times a speaker will have to make some generalizations about her audience based on the demographics that are available and known publicly. This involves conducting research and can demand a great deal of preparation, but when done well will improve the presentation as a whole. Although this may seem like stereotyping an audience (and in some ways it is), it can be an effective way to better connect with the audience during the speech. In the next chapter we will distinguish between generalizing from available information and making assumptions (that may be wrong) about the audience.

Chapter 9

Diversity and Inclusivity in Public Speaking

We can learn to see each other and see ourselves in each other and recognize that human beings are more alike than we are unalike.
—Maya Angelou

Key Concepts to Understand
Culture
Inclusivity
Ethnocentrism

In 2013, MSNBC television host Martin Bashir resigned from the network after weeks of controversy over his offensive comments about former Vice Presidential candidate Sarah Palin. Bashir was upset with political comments Ms. Palin made comparing the federal debt to slavery. So he suggested that someone should (wait for it . . .) go the bathroom in her mouth (feel free to search online for the video clips). Although not everyone may agree that he went too far, he did apologize on air in addition to resigning from the network.

There are few who would argue that we live in a more diverse and globally connected world than ever before. A report by the Public Policy Institute of California (2005) states that over 50 different languages are spoken by students in California's public schools. And according to the California Department of Education (2012) more than 2.3 million, or 37% of students spoke a language other than English at home. It is obvious that classrooms as well as workplaces are comprised of diverse groups of people. Successful public speaking creates an environment of *inclusivity* amongst the audience. *Inclusivity* means that members of the audience feel they are included rather than excluded from the setting, the speech, and the environment.

In his influential book, the anthropologist Edward T. Hall defined culture as "primarily a system for creating, sending, storing, and processing information" (Hall, 1976, p. 179). While this may seem like it has little to do with communication and even less to do with people, it is an extraordinary way of thinking about our culture. In fact, if we argue that it is our culture that guides the ways in which we communicate, then we must clearly expand our traditional thinking of culture to go far beyond our ethnicities and nationalities. Our culture can certainly include where we are from, our gender, our backgrounds, and our generations; but we can also include things like college majors and careers we work within. This idea adds a level of complexity to understanding our audience that we must recognize. We can't just make judgments about them by looking at them. Although many cultural differences are visible, there are things that are invisible as well.

REASONS TO ADOPT IT

While it may at first seem that focusing on the *differences* between audience members is counterproductive (as we have seen, we often generalize about audiences), it can be an important part of the speech preparation process. In the same way that we can learn a lot about an audience by looking at the demographics and psychographics, we can learn even more by looking at the members of an audience as a diverse and unique set of individuals. Although with a large audience this can be challenging if not impossible to do, speakers will greatly benefit from at least recognizing the diversity of the audience as a whole. There are two important reasons to understand the diversity of our audience and think about ways that speakers can make their speeches more inclusive.

WE LIVE IN A GLOBAL SOCIETY

The odds are good that anyone who speaks even occasionally in public will encounter diverse audiences. Certainly the demographics we have discussed are likely to differ between audience members, but many speakers will find themselves speaking to a broad variety of audience members in terms of gender, cultural groups, and nationalities.

In 1967, Marshall McLuhan suggested we now live in a global village; in which media technology connects us more than ever before. This is even more accurate today than when he wrote those words over forty years ago. We can now Skype with people in other nations at anytime, send emails anywhere in the world instantaneously, and work and collaborate with people in multiple nations in real-time. Most college graduates today will be working in a more complex, diverse, and global society than any generation before them ever has.

In addition to the benefits of being able to speak more than one language, workers will need to be able to understand and empathize with diverse cultures of people even within the United States.

WE LIVE IN A DIVERSE SOCIETY

The 2010 census revealed some dramatic changes in the cultural landscape of the United States (www.census.gov). Overall, the U.S. population grew, but the largest growth was of people who consider themselves to be of Hispanic or Latino origins. While this group represents just over 16% of the U.S. population, the *growth* of this group is over 40% nationwide. In California, this group represents over 37% of the population and has seen a growth rate of 27%. By comparison in California, all other cultural groups combined saw only a one and a half percent increase from 2000 to 2010. This data illustrates the rapid changes in the cultural landscape of the nation.

As we have discussed elsewhere in this book, language is only part of the differences that exist between cultures. We also have nonverbal communication differences that can make communication between members of different cultures a challenge at times.

Another cultural group that has changed dramatically are members of different generations. Many writers have given each generation their own catchy names (author/artist Douglas Coupland named people my age *Generation X* in his 1991 book). Although not all agree on the specific ages that define each generation, it is useful to think of the collective members of certain age groups as their own unique cultures. Census data in 2010 reports that more people in the US are over the age of 65 than ever before. The number of people in this group has increased at a "faster rate (15.1 percent) than the total U.S. population (9.7 percent)" (p. 1). The report also states that as a percentage of overall Americans, the older population increased and those 65 and older now represent 13 percent of America. So you can see that another way that our nation is becoming more diverse is in the form of age diversity.

An additional illustration of diversity can include economic and financial standing (what sociologists often refer to as socioeconomic status). An audience comprised of members of diverse social groups and different levels of income will clearly have a broad range of different backgrounds and experiences, and oftentimes varied ways of thinking about issues. After all, not everyone in America grew up with video games, cars, smart phones, or even homes.

Speaking of cell phones, another form of diversity you may encounter in your audience is their experience and understanding of technology. Certainly engineers need to keep this in mind when speaking to members of other career fields. But anytime an audience is gathered to hear a speech, there may be broad differences in how much they understand and use technology. I recently heard a speech in my class where the speaker asked the audience to tweet their concerns to our local politicians. Only about half of the class was using Twitter, and as a result his call to action was lost on half of the audience.

There are many great ways that speakers can display an understanding of a diverse audience and make sure everyone feels welcome and included in the speech. It begins by being sensitive to the audience and showing them that you are there because you have a message that you think will benefit them. With a little bit of preparation, speakers can be inclusive of all audience members. Here are three things speakers should try to do in all speeches.

AVOID STEREOTYPES & PREJUDICES

I know that most speakers, who are trying to make a good impression, will do their best to avoid stereotypes in their speeches. However, the reality is that there are often hidden stereotypes and prejudices that we all have inside our heads, that influence how we speak and interact with others (Sherman, Sherman, Percy, & Soderberg, 2013). While it is easy to suggest that we just turn those off, research shows we often can't do that. However, effective speakers do have an obligation to at least try to avoid using them in speaking. Additionally, it is possible for all of us to learn to reduce our biases through a learning process called *counter-prejudicial training* (Calanchini, Gonsalkorale, Sherman, & Klauer, 2013). So really, we have no excuse to use stereotypes in our speaking.

Avoid Assumptions

It may seem strange to suggest that an effective speaker avoid assumptions about an audience after we have talked about generalizing about the audience using demographics. But there is a difference between *generalizing* (which is always based on characteristics about the audience) and *assuming*, which is based on the unknown. Here are some examples: If I know that everyone in my audience is a college student, there are some generalizations that I can make about college students (they have to study, do homework, buy books, register for classes, etc.). However, I should not assume that everyone has purchased the book, has actually studied, or had done their homework.

Avoid Ethnocentrism

Another way that we can illustrate more inclusivity in our public speaking is to avoid **ethnocentrism**. This is a term that is often used to describe our cultural or ethnic biases (both conscious and unconscious) that occur when speakers view the world from the perspective of their own cultural group as one of superiority or idealism over other groups. This results in a way of thinking that views other groups as being unequal to and often inferior to one's own group. It is a sort of cultural favoritism that was evident in the 19th century (Sumner, 1906), but still exists today.

CHOOSE LANGUAGE CAREFULLY

Although I have already discussed language use (see Chapter 3), here I will remind readers of the connotative influence of words on the effectiveness of a speech. For example, when talking about law enforcement officials an inclusive speaker would say police officers not policemen. According to a report by the U.S. Department of Justice, about 20% of law enforcement offices nationwide are women (Langton, 2010). Similarly when talking about firefighting, don't say *firemen*, say fire fighters. When suggesting the audience speak with a medical doctor, do not use only gender specific pronouns. Examples of these gender specific pronouns include referring to a cardiologist (a heart surgeon) as "he" (my cardiologist is a woman) or talking about nurses and using only "she" (some registered nurses are men). Instead, use a combination of "he" or "she" (as you may have noticed, I have done in this text) or use both pronouns such as: "When you speak to your doctor, ask him or her . . ."

NONVERBAL

We have also already addressed the topic of nonverbal communication, and readers should revisit Chapter 4. However, there are some things that effective speakers can do nonverbally to let their audience see that all are welcome and included in the speech. The first is eye contact. An inclusive speaker tries to make eye contact with everyone in the audience and doesn't intentionally avoid people when controversial topics are being discussed. Obviously this is easier said than done, because we may not even know we are avoiding certain people (many students when nervous will look at the instructor far more than the rest of the class). Another aspect of nonverbal communication is the use of physical space. Research has found that when communicating across different cultures, violating the norms related to specific cultures (such as touching someone in the audience or even just getting too close to them) can negatively influence their perceptions of the speaker (McCroskey, Sallinen, Fayer, Richmond, & Barraclough, 1996). Many speakers will shake hands with audience members prior to a speech and failing to do that in a way that makes all audience members feel included and welcomed will not lead to signs of inclusivity. For example, do not shake hands with only the men (or only the women) in the audience, but be certain to connect with many of your listeners.

SUMMARY

Although this chapter/section has just served as an introduction to diversity and inclusivity in public speaking, it should provide the reader a framework for continuing to think about and discuss the ways in which we can become more effective speakers that make audience members feel welcomed and included in our presentations. And ultimately will be more influenced by our words.

REFERENCES

Angelou, Maya from Schnall, M. (2013). *What will it take to make a woman president?* Berkeley, CA: Seal Press.

California Department of Education. (2012). Statewide English learners by language and grade. (2010–11). DataQuest. Retrieved from http://data1.cde.ca.gov/dataquest/

Public Policy Institute of California http://www.ppic.org/content/pubs /report/R_405CJR.pdf

McLuhan, M. (1964). *Understanding media.* New York, NY: Mentor.

U.S. Census Bureau. (2010). U.S. Census Data. Retrieved from http://www.census.gov/2010census/data/

U.S. Census Bureau. (2010). *The older population: 2010 Census briefs.* Retrieved from http://www.census.gov/prod/cen2010/briefs /c2010br-09.pdf

Coupland, D. (1991). *Generation X: Tales for an accelerated culture.* New York, NY: St. Martin's Press.

Hall, E. T., & Hall, M. R. (1976). *Understanding cultural differences: Germans, French and Americans.* Boston, MA: Intercultural Press.

Sherman, S. J., Sherman, J. W., Percy, E. J., & Soderberg, C. K. (2013). Stereotype development and formation. In D. Carlston (Ed.), *Oxford handbook of social cognition* (pp. 548–574). New York, NY: Oxford University Press.

Calanchini, J., Gonsalkorale, K., Sherman, J. W., & Klauer, K. C. (2013). Counter-prejudicial training reduces activation of biased associations and enhances response monitoring. *European Journal of Social Psychology, 43*, 321–325.

Sumner, W. G. (1906). *Folkways: A study of the sociological importance of usages, manners, customs, mores, and morals.* New York, NY: Mentor.

Langton, L. (2010). Women in law enforcement, 1987–2008. *Crime Data Brief. Bureau of Justice Statistics.* Retrieved from http://www.bjs.gov /content/pub/pdf/wle8708.pdf

McCroskey, J. C., Sallinen, A., Fayer, J. M., Richmond, V. P., & Barraclough, R. A. (1996). Nonverbal immediacy and cognitive learning: A cross-cultural investigation. *Communication Education, 45*, 200–211.

Chapter 10

Informative Speaking

Education is the kindling of a flame, not the filling of a vessel.
—Socrates

Key Concepts to Understand
Definition of Informative Speeches
Importance of Informative Speeches
Types of Informative Speeches
Guidelines of Informative Speeches
Sample Informative Speech

I will confess that I love to be informed. I read and listen to a lot of non-fiction and self-help books and audiobooks. On television, I am obsessed with the History Channel and I watch a lot of reality crime documentaries. I love to watch biographies about celebrities and even people I've never heard of before (yes, I did see the Justin Bieber movie). I guess you could say I'm an information junkie. But I don't mind at all, because I really enjoy learning something new every chance I get. So, it should come as no surprise that I enjoy informative speaking—both listening to speeches and giving them.

DEFINITION OF INFORMATIVE SPEECH

As we have done throughout this text, we begin by defining informative speaking. To inform is synonymous with to teach, educate, enlighten, explain, impart wisdom, clarify, demonstrate, illustrate, and instruct. Together, this gives us three major goals of an informative speech: to share knowledge, to increase understanding, and to provide useful material to your audience. In part, this demands that the speaker become an expert on the topic of choice. In summary, our definition of **informative speaking is:** *to teach the audience something new.*

Effective informative speeches will analyze the audience and determine what they already know, and what they would be interested in learning. The speaker should address as many of the: who, what, when, where, why, and how questions as possible in the allotted time frame.

Three Ways to Inform

There are three primary ways to approach an informative speech. Each of these can be thought of as specific goals in terms of what the audience should be able to take away from your speech.

Describe

When we deliver an informative speech with the goal of describing something to the audience, we are attempting to illustrate details and help the audience to visualize the topic in their minds.

Explain

When we deliver an informative speech with the goal of explaining something to the audience, we are attempting to help them understand in more detail or complexity the nature of the topic. This may focus on the why, or the causes and effects, or the relationships between ideas, concepts, or theories.

Demonstrate

When we deliver an informative speech with the goal of demonstrating, we are usually trying to show the audience how to do something. Great examples on television are cooking shows and home improvement shows.

THE IMPORTANCE OF INFORMATIVE SPEECHES

Informative speaking is quite common in the workplace. Many large organizations maintain training and development or organizational development departments with the primary goal of keeping employees up-to-date on current policies, issues, and skills. In addition to specific departments and individuals, many organizations expect a variety of managers to be able to train and develop their employees. Perhaps you have found yourself in this role: training a newer employee on how to fill out paperwork, use a cash register, or phone system.

Career Promotions & Raises

For those with specific interests and skills in speaking in front of groups as well as developing courses and training employees, there are many advantages to being an effective informative speaker. When I was a bank teller during college at a major bank in California, I was promoted to senior teller in part because I was able to teach new employees how to quickly use our brand new computer system. It soon became my responsibility to provide training to not only my office, but other branch offices as well. I enjoyed the opportunity to travel and the additional pay was a nice incentive. However, I think that experience influenced my decision to go into academics as well. I suspect that many organizations (in part due to so many people fearing speaking in public) have a need for employees who can teach and train others, and will be willing to pay additional bonuses for doing so.

Better Workforce Employees

Perhaps the most important benefit of having the ability to effectively teach and train employees lies in the increased productivity and efficiency that the organizations will experience. On a broad scale, a better trained, educated, and skilled workforce can provide numerous benefits for organizations. If you own a business and can effectively train the employees who work for you, it may leave you extra time to do the more important and financially rewarding tasks, such as sales, marketing, and networking. I have a friend who owns a construction business and has several employees working for him. He found it more valuable (and cost effective) to hire people with little experience and train them himself, rather than hire more experienced employees, who also wanted higher salaries. As he told me, it is easier to "teach them how to do it the right way . . . my way."

TYPES OF INFORMATIVE SPEECHES

There are six major categories of informative speeches. We have already discussed the primary goals of delivering an informative speech (describe, explain, demonstrate). Now we will look at the variety of speech topics that you may focus on. As you read through this section, think about your speech topic and use this as a guideline to help you generate ideas.

People

Informative speeches about people can be very interesting and fun to listen to. There is an abundance of people that you can choose from. This could include: historical or political figures, actors, athletes, inventors, authors, and educators to name a few. To make these speeches interesting to the audience, think about more than just biographical information and try to conduct research that examines a greater context in which this individual lived and accomplished his/her feats.

Two other common informative speeches about a person that are used in many public speaking courses are the self-introduction or the classmate introduction. Both speeches share the goal of informing the audience either about yourself or a member of your class. As an instructor, I enjoy getting to know about the people in the classroom. Speeches about people will most likely be focused on describing or explaining rather than demonstrating.

Objects

Speeches about objects include a broad category of anything that is not human. This could include inventions, technologies, works of art, film, books, or even animals to name a few. When speaking about an object, the goal can be to describe, explain, or demonstrate.

Places

Although this category can overlap with the above, here your focus is to describe a place or to talk about the history, social, or historical significance of it. This could include landmarks, national or local parks, buildings, monuments, or even bridges. Your challenge is to go beyond the obvious such as just describing it to the audience. As an example, an informative speech about the Golden Gate Bridge would be more effective with some historical, social or political information rather than just describing its beauty and location.

Events

There are so many interesting events of historical significance and on-going interest that make this type of informative speech a fascinating topic. You could talk about the Olympics, a battle during WWII, or the Boston Marathon. Similar to speeches about people, try to look beyond the obvious main points and see if you can include the social or political impact of how these events shaped and changed history. And what effects do they have on the people who participate.

Processes

The "how-to" speech is an excellent possibility as long as you are certain the information will be relevant and new to your audience. Most of us know how to make toast, many know how to change a tire, and we all can boil water. Look for processes or activities that the audience doesn't know much about. If your audience is already college students, don't tell them how to apply to college. However, if you know how to graduate in less time, that may be a speech topic that is quite valuable information to your audience.

These speeches are most often ideally suited to chronological outlining, such as the step-by-step approach to organizing your main points.

Concepts

This can be a very broad and often complex category of topic ideas. Audience analysis becomes incredibly important in choosing a topic of concept. You must fully assess how much understanding of the topic your audience currently possesses and decide how complex the information should be. Since the focus is on the abstract rather than the concrete, it may be one of the most challenging of the topic choices. Topics could include famous theories such as Einstein's theory of relativity or they could focus on more general ideologies such as the meaning of freedom in the United States.

Issues

Speeches about issues deal with problems, matters of policy, subjects of debate, and questions of morality. Keep in mind that you are not trying to persuade the audience in an informative speech, rather you are just trying to share new information. They will ultimately decide if they would like to change behavior because of the information they obtain on their own (without your influence). You can approach these speeches by providing an overview of an issue or digging deeper into the causes of certain problems. As you explore ideas for topics, think about the major debates that are taking place in your state capital, in Washington, DC, and across the globe. Newspapers and online news sources are excellent starting points for finding topics on issues. Two effective ways to organize these speeches is to follow the topical or chronological structure. If you can address the historical context of an issue, it may fit nicely into the chronological structure.

GUIDELINES FOR EFFECTIVE INFORMATIVE SPEECHES

After analyzing your audience and picking your topic, it is important to consider a few guidelines for developing effective and informative speeches. Remember that your goal is to help your audience to learn, to understand, and sometimes to apply this topic to their lives beyond the few minutes you are speaking.

Be New

By definition, informative speaking demands that the information you share with your audience teach or educate them. If the information is not new, then as a speaker you are not really achieving that goal. So, if the audience has some knowledge of your topic, look for ways to extend that knowledge by providing information that is new, controversial, and very recently discovered. With proper research, you should be able to extend the audience's awareness of your topic.

Be Specific

One of the challenges of informative speaking is the time limitation that we have in delivering our speech. As a result, it is quite often necessary to find a way to limit and focus your topic to one or several specific aspects of it. It would not be possible to cover all of the information available about the issue of human trafficking, so Lauren Smith (see her speech below) found a way to narrow it down to just several components of a relatively complex issue. The result was the audience was able to learn new information and still ground it within the context of knowledge they already had at that time.

Be Credible

It should go without saying that effective informative speaking demands that the speaker be credible. Although we will talk about this again in the persuasive speech chapter, being a credible speaker means that *the audience believes you are knowledgeable on the topic*. The best way to be credible is to use credible evidence in your speech. Make sure that the sources you are citing are reputable and credible sources (you know my opinion on wiki pages). Be sure to cite your sources and offer a reference list to audience members who would like more information. During your speech say where your sources are from, and any other details that will add to your credibility as a speaker.

Be Objective

Remember that in the informative speech, you are not trying to persuade your audience and taking a side on an issue will quickly reduce your objectivity. We can argue that all humans have some biases and therefore are never truly objective. But the field of journalism gives us a valuable framework for understanding the concept of being objective. Good reporters are supposed to present the facts without bias and let the audience make up their own minds. Many audience members will find the more objective speaker to also be more credible than those that appear biased. While having some passion for a topic is usually a good thing, don't go overboard with it to the point of attempting to sway your audience's opinions.

Be Relevant

If you are effective at becoming an "expert" on the topic, you may then find yourself struggling with narrowing down the information to make it fit within the time limits of your speech. The challenge for all speakers is to remain relevant to your audience, so that the information is interesting to them, yet stays on topic with your speech. Obviously, good audience analysis is vital to understanding what would be of interest to them and to keep focused on making it relevant. Keep your thesis in mind, and try to notice if any of the information seems to stray off topic. Also, keep your primary goal or objective at the forefront of your planning so that you can make sure you are focused and directing the speech in an effective direction. Don't include too much information so that you have to gloss over the details. Yet at the same time, don't get so detailed that the speech becomes difficult to follow along with.

Sample Speech

Following is the text of a speech delivered by Lauren Smith* in an introduction to public speaking course.

*Used with permission

Human Trafficking

How many of you have ever seen the movie *Taken*, featuring Liam Neeson and Maggie Grace? Two American teenage girls get kidnapped by Albanian human traffickers for prostitution all while beating the girls into submission and making them drug dependent. *Taken* is a perfect example of a human trafficking situation, even though it is a bit dramatic and the end result is very unlikely. Human trafficking is the third largest crime industry (following illegal drugs and arms trafficking).

Today I am here to discuss what human trafficking is, whom it affects, and what we can do to put an end to it.

According to the United Nations Office of Drugs and Crime, human trafficking is defined as an individual recruitment, transportation, transfer, harbouring or receipt of persons, by means of the threat or use of force or other forms of abduction, of fraud, of deception, of the abuse of power or of a position of vulnerability or of the giving or receiving of payments or benefits to achieve the consent of a person having control over another person, for the purpose of exploitation. Exploitation shall include, at a minimum, the exploitation of the prostitution of others or other forms of sexual exploitation, forced labour or services, slavery or practices similar to slavery, servitude or the removal of organs (United Nation Office of Drug and Crime, 2013).

As scary as that sounds, human trafficking is becoming more and more popular, but there are still a large number of people who are unsure of the facts behind this horrible slave trade that is taking over America.

Typically, traffickers recruit women and children through deceptive means including falsified employment advertisements for domestic workers, waitresses, and other low-skilled work. Traffickers include those involved in highly sophisticated networks of organized crime and may be as close to home as a relative to the victim.

Globally, the average cost of a slave is $90; yet very young girls and virgins sell at much higher costs at the minimum of $2,000.

According to some estimates, approximately 80% of trafficking involves sexual exploitation, and 19% involves labor exploitation.

There are approximately 20–30 millions slaves in the world today.

The victims are held captive in terrible conditions. Many victims are trapped in a house with about 30 other victims and are forced to live with very little food and in very unsanitary conditions. In most cases, it is very easy to spot a trafficking home; because typically you will see several cars pull up to these homes on a daily basis. And, most importantly, there will be dark curtains or sheets in the windows, never exposing their crimes.

Now, having a firm idea of what human trafficking is, one may wonder who qualifies for abduction. According to the U.S. State Department, 600,000 to 800,000 people are trafficked across international borders every year. More than 70 percent are female and half are children. Between 14,500 and 17,500 people are trafficked into the US each year.

The average age a teen enters the sex trade in the US is 12 to 14 years old. Many victims are runaway girls who were sexually abused as children. Unfortunately, California harbors three of the FBI's 13 highest child sex trafficking areas in the nation: Los Angeles, San Francisco, and San Diego.

According to the Tolerance, Equality, and Awareness Movement, also known as TEAM, "Women and children as young as 14 have been trafficked from Mexico to Florida and forced to have sex with as many as 130 clients per week in a trailer park. These women were kept hostage through threats and physical abuse, and were beaten and forced to have abortions. One woman was locked in a closet for 15 days after trying to escape." And, for a story a little closer to home, "In Fresno, California, Hmong gang members have kidnapped girls between the ages of 11 and 14 and forced them into prostitution. The gang members would beat and rape them into submission. These girls were trafficked within the United States and traded between other Hmong communities." (Surfus, 2009–2012)

After so much depressing information, I'm glad to report that there are several organizations that have formed in the past 10 years to stop human trafficking and sexual exploitation. Just within the last two years, many celebrities have started a campaign against human trafficking and sexual exploitation.

According to *Vanity Fair*, "Even as celebrity activists such as Emma Thompson, Demi Moore, and Mira Sorvino raise awareness about commercial sex trafficking, survivor Rachel Lloyd publishes her memoir *Girls Like Us*, and the Senate introduces a new bipartisan bill for victim support, the problem proliferates across continents, in casinos, on streets, and directly into your mobile device." (Collins, 2011) Some of the most popular organizations against human trafficking are POGO and the Polaris Project. But even religious organizations have joined the cause, such as the Coalition of Catholic Organizations against Human Trafficking.

Conclusion
As nervous as I might have been to stand in front of all of you today, hoping to educate you in one of the fastest growing criminal activities, I stand here feeling accomplished that I was able to spread knowledge in hopes that if you ever suspect a human trafficking situation, you may save a life.

SUMMARY

Informative speaking is an important and challenging skill to possess. Many occupations will require one to conduct informative presentations to outside groups. Although there are differing specific goals to informative speaking, the overarching goal is to teach or educate the audience. Like all speeches, having a clear purpose and goal increases the success of the speech.

Chapter 11

Ceremonial Speaking

*The fame of heroes owes little to the extent of their conquests
and all to the success of the tributes paid to them.*
—Jean Genet

Key Concepts to Understand
Definition of Ceremonial Speeches
Occasions of Typical Ceremonial Speeches
Types of Ceremonial Speeches
Guidelines of Ceremonial Speeches
Sample Ceremonial Speech

Most of us will be asked by a friend, family member, or coworker at some point in our lives to give a ceremonial speech, a toast, or a eulogy. When the speech is done well, it becomes an important part of these special occasions that serve to bring people together around a common theme and emotional connection. This can include the joy of matrimony, the memory of a loved one, the appreciation and accomplishment of a friend or coworker, or the love of family. These events often become the most memorable times of our lives, and the thoughtful words of loved ones can make them even more special.

SPECIAL OCCASIONS

Before we define ceremonial speaking, first let's think of all of the special occasions in life where we expect to hear speeches. Have you spoken on any of the following special occasions?

- Christenings
- Bar/Bat Mitzvahs
- Quinceañeras
- Weddings
- Baby Showers
- Promotions
- Awards
- Tributes

- Births
- Certain Birthdays
- Graduation
- Reunions
- Anniversaries
- Retirements
- Funerals
- Etc.

CEREMONIAL SPEAKING DEFINED

The best way to look at what a speech has in common with all of these special occasions is to think of the goal you have when giving the speech. If it is a wedding, your goal is to celebrate and share in the love of the happy couple. If you are speaking at a funeral, your goal is to share in the memory of the person who has passed away. If we give a speech after receiving an award, we often show our thanks to all those who helped in our achievement (watch the Academy Awards™ shows). In all of these cases (celebrate, share love, remember, show thanks), we are sharing emotions with our audience. The same ideas are true when giving a **tribute speech**:

We are trying to connect with the audience on an emotional level.

Most importantly, keep in mind that we are not just providing information about the person, but you must think about how this audience can feel an emotional connection to the person/people/occasion through your use of language in your speech.

Tribute Speech

The most common ceremonial speech in public speaking classes is probably the *speech of tribute*. In this type of speech, the speaker has the primary goal of sharing and connecting emotions with the audience and explaining why this person is worthy of praise. As you recall from the last chapter, in the informative speech you were looking for ways to educate and inform your audience. However in this speech, education and information is secondary to sharing something of value. This could include things like why this person is unique, has overcome adversity, has inspired people, and is someone that the audience should admire as well (even if they have never before heard of this individual). Some great examples of how this is commonly done are in Hollywood films. Think of the movies you have seen about ordinary people who have overcome adversity to do extraordinary things, oftentimes based on true stories. These movies seem to be a staple of industry, and can be found playing in every movie theatre at almost any time. When these movies are successful, it is usually because they are written to not just tell us about the person, but to help us feel an emotional connection with the person (or team, or animal, or other character). A few of my favorites are *The Pursuit of Happyness* with Will Smith, *Braveheart* with Mel Gibson, and *Remember the Titans* with Denzel Washington.

These speeches do not have to focus on only the individual; they can focus on a team, as was done to some degree in the movie *Miracle*, about the 1984 USA Olympic Hockey Team, or an occupation (there have been many tributes to firefighters over the years), or even an animal. There have been some great (and not so great) movies about real-life extraordinary animals including a family dog named *Marley*, a horse during WWI in Steven Spielberg's *War Horse*, some whales stuck under ice in Alaska in *Big Miracle*, and a dolphin that lost its tale in *Dolphin Tale* with Morgan Freeman. Several of which have brought me to tears on more than one occasion. (I wonder why there aren't true story movies about cats? . . .)

Topics

As we just discussed these tribute speeches can focus on people, but you can also pay tribute to places and things as well. If you pay tribute to places or things, your focus will be slightly different. When the subject of a tribute speech is not human, the focus must be more directed towards the ceremonial and symbolic values of that subject. For example, if I am paying tribute to my grandfather it would make perfect sense for me to talk about what a thoughtful, caring, supportive, and extraordinary person he was. However, if I am going to pay tribute to a superhero, it is going to sound unrealistic, possibly cheesy, and slightly strange to talk about how great a man this fictional cartoon character is. However, if we look at the power and influence that fictional characters have on popular culture and society, it would be fair to say that this character *represents* some very powerful qualities. Think of these qualities as symbolic values, not so much as human characteristics. One of my all-time favorite comic strips was Calvin & Hobbes and as such was the subject of my ceremonial speech in my public speaking class long ago. I chose to discuss how Calvin (and his alter-ego Hobbes) represented some great qualities that inspired readers to try to find in their own lives. My three main points were the three things that I felt Calvin possessed and that he reminded us we all should strive for and included: Individualism (he reminds us to be ourselves and forge our own path in life), Inquisitive (with his curiosity and wild imagination, he is not afraid to ask why, to question everything, and to take nothing in life *as-is*), and Innocence (everything he approached was always from a new perspective; he seemed to revel in the unknown and the delight of discovery on a daily basis).

Organization

The basic structure of the ceremonial speech is similar to the informative speech in that there are three major sections: Introduction, Body, and Conclusion. As we discussed before, the introduction should include a clear thesis sentence that lets the audience know exactly what the speech will be focusing on while paying tribute to this person, place, or thing. As always, the goal of the introduction is to grab the audience's attention and captivate their interest so that they can't wait to hear more about this speech topic.

Each of the main points in the body of the speech should center on the ceremonial values that you are using to pay tribute to this subject. Each main point should be explained or defined and then supported with expert testimony (quotes from reputable sources who know the subject well or have some other quality that makes them knowledgeable on the subject). Oftentimes, support and quotes from more than one expert will strengthen the arguments in the speech. Between the main points the speaker should transition smoothly so that there is good flow and organization to the speech.

Finally, the conclusion should wrap up the speech and most importantly leave the audience with something memorable. Oftentimes it will make sense to tie into the opening of the speech, but it is not always necessary.

Readers should take some time to review the chapter on public speaking and the options to organizing your speech before you begin writing the outline.

Guidelines

There are four important things that you can do to make your ceremonial speeches more effective, enjoyable, and memorable.

1. Connect with your audience

    Look for themes, memories, and examples that many in the audience can identify with. If your audience doesn't know the person well, but are all college students, can you connect the speech to some of the shared and common experiences that college students have?

2. Use powerful language

    As we discussed in the chapter on verbal communication and language (Chapter 3), words are powerful. In describing how good a person is, you may want to turn to your thesaurus and see if you can incorporate much more dynamic language into the speech (try also: decent, respectable, moral, virtuous, noble, worthy, wholesome, kind, warm, honorable, etc.).

3. Share stories

    While stories are valuable in all speeches, they are almost a requirement for ceremonial speeches. If you were paying tribute to someone, remembering someone, or even making a toast at a wedding, telling stories about the subject will connect the audience on an emotional level. If the story has emotion in it (such as humor), it becomes even more powerful.

4. Deliver with passion

    Obviously if you are paying tribute to someone whom you admire, you should be able to show that admiration in your language, voice, body language, and overall delivery of the speech. Sometimes a passionate speech delivery does more to connect with the audience on an emotional level than the language and stories do on their own.

Sample

Below is a tribute speech by Methi Satyanarayana* on a beautiful statue located in France. Notice how she is able to discuss the symbolism and the significant representation of this work of art in a way that makes the listener feel not just informed but inspired. As a visual aid, Methi brought in a photograph of the statue that she had printed on a photographic digital printer to a size of about 2 feet by 3 feet. As a supplement to the

*Used with permission

language used in the speech, the picture helped the audience to see and really understand the unique qualities of the statue. Perhaps after reading the speech you will also feel a desire to see it in person.

I. Introduction
Children are constantly told stories about heroes such as Sir Galahad, Hercules, and Odysseus. These famous heroes all had something extraordinary that made them capable of great feats. But not all heroes have to be demi-gods or even gifted. Sometimes heroes can be normal people in extraordinary circumstances.

II. Thesis
Today I want to celebrate the Burghers of Calais, captured by the iconic statue by Auguste Rodin, for defying the artistic norms of the time and for being a symbol of ultimate sacrifice.
Transition: Let's start with the story behind the statue.

III. Main Points
A. Background
1. Why the statue was commissioned
   a. After Franco-Prussian war French Gov. wants to instill nationalism by memorializing French Patriots through building statues
2. History behind the Burghers of Calais
   a. 1895, Statue commemorates event in the 100 years war
   b. In the year 1347, King Edward III besieges Calais for 11 months → famine and Calais near destruction
   c. Orders six citizens of the city to carry the key to the city while dressed in peasant garb with nooses around their necks
3. The Burghers: Eustache de Saint-Pierre & five others
   a. Influential respected citizens, had families
   b. Eustache de Saint-Pierre volunteers first
   c. According to Cornell University professor, Richard Swedberg, "Edward III wanted them to be executed but the Queen intervened on their behalf. As a result of her efforts, the lives of the Burghers were saved."
Transition: While Rodin was originally supposed to create a statue of only Eustache de Saint-Pierre his statue ended up looking very different.

B. Rodin's vision vs. the expected style
1. Swedberg says "The typical statue [at the time] was often of an individual; it was allegorical in nature; and the whole thing was mounted on a pedestal and given the shape of a pyramid."

    2. The Burghers of Calais varies from convention
      a. In a square formation
      b. Group of unique individuals
      c. Meant to be viewed at ground level
      d. Looks emotional and not heroic in the traditional sense
Transition: It is this unique composition that makes Rodin's statue so rich with symbolism.

  C. Symbolism of sacrifice
    a. Visually a symbol of sacrifice and the reality of heroism
    b. The Calouste Gulbenkian Museum says that "Each of these men have their own physical identity and psychological characteristics, which explain their different states of mind on facing martyrdom."
    c. Certain attributes tie them together
      i. Enlarged hands and feet
      ii. Bent emaciated bodies
      iii. Realistic not jubilant facial expressions
    d. Their soul pushes them onward, but their feet refuse to walk." —Rodin
Transition: It is because these men experienced very human emotions and were still willing to die for their city that they are truly heroes.

IV. Conclusion: The Burghers of Calais broke artistic convention and captured the immense sacrifice those men were willing to make. Hopefully, you see that heroes can live among us as normal people. When we are faced with difficult trials our own inner hero is released within us.

V. References

"Auguste Rodin." *Musée Rodin.* N.p., n.d. Web. 5 May 2013.

"Jean d'Aire, Burgher of Calais." *Museu Calouste Gulbenkian.* Calouste Gulbenkian Foundation, 2008. Web. 5 May 2013.

Miller, Joan Vita, and Gary Marotta. *Rodin: The B. Gerald Cantor Collection.* New York: The Metropolitan Museum of Art, 1986. Digital text.

"Rodin and Claudel: the Sculptor, his Muse and the Musee." Blog. *Polloplayer. Wordpress.* N.p., 27 Sept. 2011. Web. 4 May 2013.

Swedberg, Richard. "Auguste Rodin's The Burghers of Calais: The Career of a Sculpture and its Appeal to Civic Heroism." *Theory Culture Society* 22.45 (2005): 64. *Sagepub.* Web. 4 May 2013.

SUMMARY

Paying tribute to someone or something is one of the most common speeches in our lives. Most of us will have multiple opportunities to listen to and deliver these types of speeches beyond the classroom. If you keep in mind that your goal should always be to share emotions with your audience and you follow the guidelines in this chapter while finding your own unique approach to organizing the speech, you should be able to connect with your audience each and every time.

REFERENCES

Genet, J. (1986). *Prisoner of love.* Paris: Gallimard.

Chapter 12

Persuasive Speaking

Too many people spend money they haven't earned, to buy things they don't want, to impress people they don't like.
—Will Rogers

Key Concepts to Understand
Definition of Persuasion
Logos
Pathos
Ethos
Fallacies

While conducting research for this chapter, I began searching for the answer to a fairly simple question: How many persuasive messages do Americans receive each day? Surprisingly, this was not easy to find. My first results came up with people claiming that each day we were targeted with 3,000 to 5,000 persuasive appeals (in the form of advertisements). What was interesting was NONE of these websites offered any evidence of this statistic. Therefore, I have to question it.

Then I decided to find out for myself. Today, I counted 128 persuasive appeals. There were probably more, but I didn't notice them. I watched some television, read through the college newspaper, then watched a DVD. While that might seem like a small number, it occurs to me that over a year, or a decade, or even my lifetime, . . . it's a lot!

I think it's fair to say, that every day, we are bombarded with persuasive messages.

WHAT IS PERSUASION?

Persuasion is *the act of changing another's attitudes, beliefs, opinions, and/or behaviors*. Notice a key term of that definition is to cause change. Attempting to change one's behaviors, but failing is NOT persuasion. It was a "failed attempt at persuasion."

Persuasion versus Information. There is a difference between informing an audience member and persuading them. Informative speaking is educating your audience. If they happen to change some behaviors based on the information, then they were not necessarily persuaded. The reason they changed behavior has to do with the information, NOT the speaker. Persuasion is caused by a speaker. Usually because the speaker appeals to the audience, thus causing them to change.

HOW TO PERSUADE
IN A SPEECH CLASS

You begin with an **issue**. An issue is *something that has two or more sides*. At the very least, the two sides are for and against, or PRO and CON. There certainly can be more than two sides to an issue, usually in the form of some variation of the for or against position (e.g., for social security reform, there are numerous sides and opinions on the issue).

There are three types of persuasive topics or questions. Those are questions of fact, value, and policy.

Questions of Fact concern what is true or not true. Aren't all facts true? Not necessarily. We tend to believe that facts are true. But, haven't there been facts that we thought were true, but later found out to be false? Of course, and that is why there are often persuasive speeches and debates on questions of fact. In fact (pun intended), there are plenty of books, movies, and television shows that attempt to persuade us to believe some facts are true or untrue.

Questions of Value concern what we think is good or bad, right or wrong, just or unjust, fair or unfair. Since these are the issues that many people hold near and dear to their hearts, their faith, and their way of life, these are often contentiously debated and argued.

Questions of Policy concern things that are rules, laws, and/or regulations. These are the issues that affect us the most. After all, the laws and policies of our government often dictate how we live our daily lives and what we can or cannot do. So it should come as no surprise that these questions are not only contentiously debated, but oftentimes considered the most important topics of ours lives (think of the issues that you are most concerned with).

Once you have decided on a topic, found the issue, researched the current policies on that issue, and decided how you would like to change the current policies (notice that IS the process of putting together your speech topic—see below). The three types are: Logos (Logical Appeals), Pathos (Emotional Appeals), and Ethos (Speaker Credibility).

LOGOS

Logical arguments are ideally suited for an audience that is prepared and motivated to analyze your arguments and evaluate your message. Logical arguments use evidence to support the claims. The structure of a logical argument is as follows: (Rhetoric, by Aristotle)

1. Claim
2. Evidence
3. Conclusion

How Do I Decide on a Topic?

So, you have to pick a "policy" topic. Now what? Well, you begin with research. Let's say you have decided on "something with education." Well, that isn't narrow enough. There must be thousands of issues on education. So, keep going. . . .

Something with education > cost of education > cost of higher education > financial aid > federal loans > not enough > need more > government should help us MORE.

There, you have a question of policy: Should the government provide more financial aid for college students? That works. But, which government? OK, the federal.

Now, you need to become an expert on the current policy. How much federal financial aid does the government provide? I bet you can

---

(continued)

How Do I Decide on a Topic? (continued)

find that one out easily (www.fafsa.ed.gov). Here you will see that the subsidized loan amounts (meaning the interest is paid while you are in school) are less than the cost of attending college. Here is an older policy:

If you're a dependent undergraduate student, each year you can borrow up to $7,500 (for the 2007–08 academic year) if you're a first-year student enrolled in a program of study that is at least a full academic year. No more than $3,500 of this amount may be in subsidized loans. http://studentaid.ed.gov/PORTALSWebApp/students/english/studentloans.jsp

So, your speech could suggest that the numbers be raised. You can decide how much on your own, or do some more research on the Internet, and you just might find that there are some elected officials who have already suggested this before. Or you could suggest we lobby someone to enact this legislation.

You still need to think about the objections to this. (What . . . college students object to **more** money?) While many support the idea, the question of WHO will pay for this extra money and where will it come from is a legitimate one to ask. In fact, you still may need to persuade the audience to support cutting the money from something else or raising taxes to cover this expense.

Let's analyze that. You begin with a claim. You support that claim with evidence (discussed below) and from that you draw a conclusion. Let's try one. Claim: We should lower the drinking age from 21 to 18. Evidence: You can join the military at 18 and die for your country. Conclusion: Therefore, you should also be able to drink (when you join the military and die for your country). What is the problem with this argument? First, there is no logical connection between the military and drinking. Why would one NEED alcohol to join the military? It may help, but it isn't a reason. Second, is there any logical reason in that argument why 18 is the appropriate age for drinking? No. Lastly, military personnel can drink alcohol when they are outside of the US even if they are not 21. So, we need to find a better argument. Let's work through it again. What evidence would support that the drinking age should be lowered? Ideally, we need evidence that shows having the drinking age at 21 does more harm than good. If you could find evidence that is credible and shows that by having a 21-year-old drinking age, college students in particular are more likely to abuse alcohol, then we would have a good example.

Evidence. There are three types of evidence. 1) You can use data and/or statistics if you have done the research yourself or you can cite data from a credible source. 2) You can use narrative, which are personal stories from people who have experienced the issue firsthand. If you personally interview a soldier who has served in Iraq, you would have some good narrative for your topic. Oftentimes, the farther away from the original source you are, the less credible it becomes. 3) And finally, you can use expert testimony, meaning you cite another credible expert as a source.

However, there are <u>four</u> things that make expert testimony credible. What is the source's *experience*? Does your source have education, training, and/or *credentials* that show his/her expertise? Has the source earned a *reputation* as being credible? Is your source *affiliated* with someone or something that your audience already considers credible?

PATHOS

Appealing to one's sense of emotion can be a powerful form of persuasion. Advertisers do it all the time because it works. There are essentially two types of emotional appeals.

Positive Emotional Appeals. Usually try to get us to feel good, happy, warm, loving, and upbeat about the issue. *This is most often used in sales. My favorite lines I've been told while shopping for cars: This car is sporty, This is a fun car, You look good in this car, Women will be attracted to you in this car (really . . . and no, it didn't work).*

Negative Emotional Appeals. Usually in the form of scaring us or making us feel guilty. However, they work. Can you think of a recent advertisement that you saw that was trying to scare you into buying a product?

Do they work? The answer is, oftentimes, yes. Especially if they will reinforce the emotions we already have. However, research shows they are less effective at changing our emotions (see the classic work on persuasion by Petty & Cacioppo).

ETHOS

Aristotle wrote in great detail about **ethos** or the ethics and credibility of a speaker (see the University of Tennessee's website for a detailed description of his life and writings). There are essentially four things that you as a modern day persuasive speaker can do to add credibility to your speech.

1. *Use Credible Research*
   What makes your sources credible? The answer depends on the audience again. What is credible to one group may not be so credible to another. Think of newspapers as an example. What are some of the newspapers you find credible? Perhaps the Los Angeles Times comes to mind. What about the San Luis Obispo Tribune? Which do you find more credible between the two? How about the Mustang Daily? Is that newspaper credible? What defines credibility is the reputation the source has earned. If you have a source from Harvard University, we will likely view that as a credible source, because in the United States we tend to hold Harvard in high esteem. The university has an excellent reputation.

   Now, think about the bias that a newspaper may have. Without overanalyzing and getting into a philosophical debate, wouldn't you agree that all newspapers are somewhat biased? Everyone of us has our own biases and all we can do is hope to set those aside and do our best to be neutral. But in reality, we often cannot do that. When you are called to jury duty, the judge asks you if you can set aside your biases and make a fair and just decision based on the law. You are NOT asked if you have NO biases. We ALL do.

   It may surprise you to realize the most credible (as in least biased) newspaper of the three is the Mustang Daily. After all, it is the ONLY newspaper that is not at the mercy of a for-profit corporation and paid by advertisers. Would a Fox News affiliate have to think very carefully if they had a news story that was negative about Rupert Murdoch (the man who owns the majority of Fox News)? Aristotle brought up a good point: To be an ethical speaker, you must first recognize that you have certain biases, and then rather than attempt to hide that from your audience, you must admit your biases and then illustrate why they are not interfering with your message.

   And most importantly, to add credibility to your speech, remember to *cite the source of each and every idea that is not your own during the speech each and every time that you use it*.

2. *Deliver Well*
   Wouldn't you agree that the confidence and competence with

which you deliver your speech would add to your credibility? Practice so that you sound confident.

3. ***Connect with Your Audience***
If you were asked to go back to your high school and talk to the students about college, you probably wouldn't dress like a business professional. Think about when you were in high school. Would it have been harder to relate to or identify with a college student wearing a suit and tie?

4. **Show Your Similarity to Your Audience**
It may seem sad to you, but there are people out there in America who really do identify with and relate to television celebrities. That is why they are paid so much to be spokespeople for products. It does sell product. Once Oprah Winfrey told her viewers they should buy the book *East of Eden* by John Steinbeck. That night so many people went online and ordered the book that the publisher literally ran out (some reports estimated that over 50,000 copies were ordered in a 24-hour period). It became impossible to find a copy of the book anywhere in the US. The publisher had to reprint the book to keep up with demand. In the end, the book club resulted in 1.7 million copies sold (Nielsen).

It may surprise you to know how many celebrities do television commercials but don't show their faces. Instead, they are the voice-over or narrations. Here are just a few: Lowes Home Improvement Stores uses Gene Hackman; Cingular used to use Charlie Sheen; Blockbuster uses Alec Baldwin; Cadillac uses Gary Sinise; Pizza Hut uses Queen Latifah; and Go RVing uses Tom Selleck.

Speech Structures

There are several common organizational structures for persuasive speeches. The basic "problem-solution" is an effective organization structure for many public policy speech topics. In this format, the speaker begins with showing the audience a problem that directly affects their lives. The speaker then lays out a solution to that problem in the form of an improved public policy that will fix (or at least help solve some of) the problem.

Sample Outline of Problem-Solution

You should follow the same format as the other speeches.

  I. Introduction (use a good, strong, catchy intro that grabs your audience, and at the same time establishes YOUR credibility).

  II. Thesis (preview the speech, but no need to be too direct. You should summarize the problem and your solution and hint at how the audience can help, without saying something as direct as, "I'm here to persuade you.").

  III. Body (a great option)

    A. Problem

      1. Explain what the problem is, for whom, and use lots and lots of details. (who, what, when, where, why, how)

    B. Solution

      1. Explain why THIS solution is the BEST solution. You may need to deal with some objections and the opposition here.

  IV. Conclusion. Must include your persuasive appeals and a clear direct call to action that tells the audience what you want them to do and when and how and why it will work. Remember (again), it MUST be a public policy solution.

  V. References

Although that may seem short right now, keep in mind that you will probably need to have a lot of detail about the problem, explaining it multiple ways. Furthermore, you will most likely need to have a lot of detail about the solution and why it is the best solution, how it could be implemented, and what obstacles will be overcome. You probably need to have a number of appeals rather than just one or two.

In some cases, it would make sense to add a third section to the speech and discuss some of the causes of the problems. This requires that you (a) have time to discuss the problems, and (b) understand and can explain the causes of the problems (with evidence).

Monroes Motivated Sequence

Another useful organizational style for your persuasive speech was developed by Professor Alan H. Monroe of Purdue University and is now called Monroe's Motivated Sequence (Ehninger, Monroe, & Gronbeck, 1978). This sequence is considered by many public speaking teachers to be one of the most important organizational designs in persuasive speaking. The sequence involves organization of your speech around five steps that lead your audience toward successful persuasion.

Step One: Attention

In addition to the introduction of your speech (which also serves to gain the attention of your audience and focus them on listening to your speech), the primary goal of the first step is to focus the audience's attention on the severity and importance of your **topic** and convince them that it relates to them so they will care about it enough to listen (and eventually take action). This can be accomplished in many of the same methods that we use to open the speech with. You could make some startling statement(s) about your topic that would arouse curiosity or suspense. You could use a relevant quotation from a credible source. You could pose a question (such as a rhetorical). You could share some powerful data or statistics that illustrate the context of your topic. And finally, you could tell a dramatic story or anecdote. This step is the foundation of your argument and must be well thought out, powerful, and structured effectively.

Step Two: Need

In this step, you are trying to convince your audience that they *need* to take action and do something about this topic. Here you should begin to describe the problem(s) with the current situation and show them how and why there is a strong need for change. Your goal is to make them feel that the change is something that must take place. You want the audience to feel compelled to desire change. This can be done connecting the problems to their own lives and letting them see how serious the problem is. Clearly the speaker must provide good credible support in this section (logos as well as pathos). The speaker should also try to illustrate the problem with detailed, specific, and realistic examples. This can occur in the form of testimony as well as credible statistics, data, and research. If the speaker is successful at convincing the audience of the need for change, they will be primed and open-minded to the next step.

Step Three: Satisfaction

In step three, your goal is to show the audience that there is a way to satisfy this problem by providing them a solution. This occurs by taking the form of a detailed plan, or vision, that you will outline and explain in an effort to get the audience to want to accept your solution and take action. It is important that the speaker clearly describes the action or change that you desire the audience adopts. This plan must be explained in a way that is complete and detailed enough that the audience will be able to make a decision. Speakers will need to address all of the concerns (as reasonably possible in the time limit) that their listeners may have or be thinking about. For some speaker topics, it will be appropriate to use a demonstration (either showing it or describing it in the speech). This will serve as a model of the desired condition or state of the audience after changing the current situation. Again, using credible sources and detailed facts, figures, testimony, and expert sources are vital to persuading the audience to support this plan. If there are complex statistics and data involved, the speaker should plan to illustrate these with charts and graphs whenever possible. Since many public policies will have obvious objections, it is appropriate for the speaker to prepare counterarguments and handle the objections in the audience members' minds. Once the listeners understand the solution, they will begin to wonder how it will work for them and what they can do.

Step Four: Visualization

In this step, the speaker is now trying to get the audience to imagine exactly what their lives will be like if either (a) nothing changes or (b) the plan is adopted. Perhaps one of the most important things for speakers to do effectively in this step is be detailed, but realistic and believable. Many topics with serious problems have complex and varied solutions that, even in a perfect world, are likely to have bumps in the road to change. Although all persuasive speeches will have time limits, speakers will need to provide enough details to help the audience see the results of the solution/plan and feel that these results are possible and practical. When speakers have not done enough research into the problem, they run the risk of offering solutions that may be unrealistic and infeasible given the current state of affairs in government, the economy, and organizations. The more evidence the speaker can offer, the more likely the plan is going to be something the audience can clearly visualize.

There are three ways to get the audience to visualize the solution. The speaker must make a choice (given the likely time constraints of the speech) about which method will be most powerful for the audience. The first option is to create a positive vision approach. Here the speaker will focus on describing the situation if the solution is adopted. You should help the audience to see how much better things will be with your plan in place. If you are limited with time, and have a clear plan, this is a great approach to take. Another option is to use the method that paints the picture of a negative vision. With this approach, the speaker is trying to show the audience what life would be like if the proposed solution is rejected. Essentially, you are showing them what will happen without your plan in place. And the third option is to combine the two methods and use a contrasting vision approach. Here you would try to show the audience how great life will be with your plan in place and how awful it would be without it. Clearly, this requires more time and may not be an option in every speaking situation. However, this approach is more susceptible to the fallacies if the speaker uses too many hypothetical examples. It is important that every situation you describe as a possibility of occurring without your plan in place is supported by credible evidence and logical reasoning.

Step Five: Action

The final step involves the call to action. Here you are not only summarizing your message, but also you are now trying to get the audience to do something to make your solution become reality. The most effective calls to action are detailed, but very specific and tell the audience exactly what you want them to do or to whom they should contact, and exactly what they should say, when it should be done, etc. A good call to action should also be easy for the audience. Something as simple as providing a letter for them to sign and return to you is more likely to be successful than asking them to send it on their own. One option in this step is to make the appeals in the form of an offer or a challenge. You can begin with something small and work your way up to greater commitment. An example of this could include starting off by asking them to raise their hands if they want something better. This gets them in the habit of agreeing with you before you ask them to take further action. Some of the things that can be done as part of the appeals to action can involve using powerful quotations that inspire the audience. You can also create very detailed illustrations and descriptions that will help the audience to move forward. But most importantly, the speaker should seek to get commitment from the audience to take action. Despite all of the persuasive appeals, tricks, and techniques, don't forget that the most important is to ask for commitment. If you don't ask, they may not do anything.

As I mentioned above, many consider this to be a highly effective tool at creating and delivering persuasive speeches. Hopefully, you now feel that you have another tool to help you organize your persuasive speech to be more persuasive and effective.

AVOIDING THE FALLACIES

Fallacies are errors in reasoning. It should come as no surprise that while there are a handful of ways to make a good argument, there are many,

many more ways to screw it up. I am going to share with you the ten most common fallacies and give you an example of each one. The purpose of this information is for you to be certain you are avoiding these mistakes and use this as a "checklist" to verify that your arguments are correct.

Slippery Slope

The slippery slope fallacy occurs when we assume that taking the first step will lead to other steps, yet there is no logical reason to assume this. For example, when Californians had the option to legalize marijuana for medical use, the opposition attempted to make the following argument: If we legalize marijuana for medicinal purposes, the drug advocates will soon be able to get it legalized for all uses, and before we know it all drugs will be legal. That is a slippery slope.

Statistical Fallacies

The problem with statistics is that they are confusing. There is an old joke that goes something like this: "Research shows that 82% of all statistics are made up on the spot." I have personally seen many instances when reputable media organizations misuse statistics. Recently, *Time Magazine* ran a health report in which they reported the following alarming statistics: One child dies of malaria in Africa every 29 seconds. Someone in the world dies of TB every 18 seconds. One pregnant woman dies of complications every 60 seconds. One person is infected with HIV every 6.4 seconds. While those numbers make for dramatic statements, they are inaccurate. In fact, they are averages. A statistical average or mean is calculated by taking the estimated annual number of children who die of malaria in Africa each year and then dividing that down from days, hours, minutes, and then seconds. However, in the 58 seconds you were reading this it is false to say two children died. However, you may make these claims as long as you state "on average."

Defective Testimony

Defective, also known as false testimony, is when someone is untruthful, deceitful, or misquoted. An extreme example of this occurred when Dr. Lenore Weitzman published her book in 1995, *The Divorce Revolution: The Unexpected Social and Economic Consequences for Women and Children in America*. She claimed in her book that divorced women with children experienced a decline in their standard of living after their divorce, while the former husbands experienced a rise in their standard of living. As a result of this publicity, some states changed the way they allocate child support and alimony payments to divorced women. However, when other sociologists attempted to verify her data, they were unable to find the same results. It wasn't until 1996 that she publicly admitted her conclusions were wrong. But, by then it was too late.

Red Herring

The red herring is a diversion to move the audience away from the real issue. *Why should we worry about the amount of violence on television when so many children are injured in automobile accidents?* This is a red herring. So is, *we should lower the drinking age from 21 to 18 because you can join the military at the age of 18.*

Ad Hominem

In Latin, this translates to *against the man*. It is a personal attack. In collegiate debate, personal attacks are prohibited. One must not claim "my opponent is an idiot" but rather "my opponent has misrepresented the facts." In politics, they seem to be strongly encouraged.

Bandwagon

This is the "everybody's doing it, we should too" argument. Sometimes it begins with "California is the last state to adopt this plan . . ." However, that in and of itself is not a logical reason to adopt any plan. Perhaps the plan isn't good for us. Also, this is used with public opinion polls to persuade us. As in "eighty percent of Californians would support an increase in . . ." and the assumption is that YOU should too. There are better reasons to support or not support a public policy than everyone else does. My other favorite: We should lower the drinking age to 18, because everyone drinks anyway.

Post Hoc

This is a statistical error that occurs when a correlation is misunderstood to be the same as a cause-effect relationship. I have seen reputable media organizations misquote researchers to imply that the research found the cause when they did not. As an example, major news sources reported on the findings of a study conducted at the Maryland Medical Research Institute. The study found a correlation (meaning a relationship) between girls who ate breakfast and being slimmer (measured using Body Mass Index as a scale). This does not prove that IF a girl eats breakfast, doing so will cause her to lose weight. Yet the title of the article was misleading. It was: "Study: Breakfast, Cereal keeps girls slim." Not true. Breakfast cereal doesn't keep girls slim. Perhaps slim girls eat breakfast. Perhaps it gives the metabolism a jump-start. Perhaps they eat healthier all day. All of these were mentioned in the article, despite a misleading headline. Shame on the AP. Did I mention the funding for this particular study also came from cereal maker General Mills . . . hmmm.

Non Sequitur

In Latin this means nonsequential. The claim in the argument doesn't lead us to the conclusion. Former Cincinnati Reds owner Marge Schott once said during an ESPN interview in May 1996 while praising German dictator Adolf Hitler saying, "Everybody knows he was good at the beginning, but he just went too far."

Hasty Generalization

This is simply making too quick a judgment with too little facts. *My friend got a "D" in Teitelbaum's class, so he must be a tough teacher.* One "D" does not make a teacher tough.

Either-or

This is the mistake of assuming that only one of two possibilities is the solution. Be sure that you do enough research to consider all solutions. There is often more than just the Republican and Democratic solution floating around Congress. For example, with social security reform there are about six plans.

Use the above 10 fallacies as a checklist to make certain you don't commit any of the fallacies. For even more fun, watch a political debate and see how many of these our elected and aspiring officials commit over and over again.

Reusable Bag Persuasive Speech
Based on the Speech by Erica Dean

Introduction:

The impact of single-use plastic shopping bags on our state of California is extremely negative. The implementation of a reusable and composite shopping bag ordinance could prevent waste and litter found on streets and in storm drains within California. The use of reusable and composite bags could also prevent death of marine organisms and the destruction of their habitat. Lastly, a plastic bag requires anywhere from 10 to 100 years to begin to decompose, and never completely decomposes. Not implementing the reusable bag ordinance policy is unethical because the benefits of this ordinance outweigh the negative costs of how it affects California.

I am here today to persuade you to sign my petition to the Governor in support of a statewide ban on single-use plastic bags.

The reusable bag ordinance is the ban of the distribution of plastic bags. This means when shopping at grocery stores, pharmacies, and retailers, you have to bring a reusable bag or purchase a composite (paper) bag. This is an example of the reusable bag ordinance from San Luis Obispo County.

Every year Americans use approximately 1 billion shopping bags, which creates 300,000 tons of landfill waste. The state of California alone spends 25 million dollars transporting plastic bags to landfills each year, and another 8.5 million dollars to remove littered bags from the streets. According to International Coastal Cleanup, an organization that cleans nearly every beach along the California coast, plastic bags are one of the most common forms of waste found on California beaches. That fact should change from the present tense to past.

In California, 75 cities and counties have implemented the reusable bag ordinance, and more are constantly added. The state of California should take after these cities and counties by adopting this statute. For example, the county of San Luis Obispo, a county of 271, 969 individuals, adopted the reusable bag ordinance in 2011–2012. According to Bill Worrell, Integrated Waste Management Authority Manager in San Luis Obispo, only 2–3 percent of plastic bags were being recycled. The streets of San Luis Obispo constantly were littered with plastic bags, as well as a buildup of waste was always present in dumps. In California, a state of nearly 38 million residents, the number of plastic bags used is exponentially greater than San Luis Obispo. Not all plastic bags are disposed of correctly. Even when disposed of correctly, plastic bags are a hazard for California landfills to deal with. The problems in San Luis Obispo County are exacerbated in California because of its larger size. The simple solution to prevent further waste in our streets and further wasted tax dollars is to implement the reusable bag ordinance.

(continued)

Reusable Bag Persuasive Speech (continued)

The use of plastic bags is not only harmful to land environments, but also to marine environments. According to the sixty-forth volume of the *Marine Pollution Bulletin*, a collection of marine science articles, plastic debris in the ocean is continuing to increase and is becoming exponentially more harmful to marine life. Marine animals confuse plastic bags with prey and often eat them. For example, plastic bags floating in the water appear similar to jelly fish; as a result, turtles often eat them resulting in chocking. Another negative result is turtle's stomachs contain too much plastic and they starve because there is no room to contain anything else. Marine life can also accidentally entangle in plastic debris causing injuries. Further entanglement can result in suffocation, starvation, drowning, and increased vulnerability to injury. Volunteers participating in the annual International Coastal Cleanup event in 2008 discovered 443 animals and birds entangled or trapped by plastic debris. These annual cleanups along the coast of California are raising concerns regarding the amount of plastic in the water. If the reusable bag ordinance is implemented, there will be fewer bags in the ocean. With fewer bags in the ocean, there will be less harm to marine life. Therefore, we should implement the reusable bag ordinance. With this, we can preserve our beautiful Pacific Ocean and continue to uphold our wonderful reputation.

Furthermore, according to the U.S. National Park Service's Mote Marine Lab, plastic bags require a minimum of ten to twenty years to start the decomposition process. However, some researchers fear that plastic bags may never completely decompose, but instead turn into smaller fragments of plastic. The most common type of plastic bags, such as the bags found in grocery stores, are made of polyethylene. Polyethylene consists of long chains of ethylene monomers and is a petroleum-derived polymer, or substance that has a molecular structure built-up from a large number of similar units bonded together. Microorganisms cannot recognize polyethylene as a food source and so plastic bags made from these polymers cannot be classified as biodegradable.

While researchers found that although polyethylene cannot biodegrade, it will break down when exposed to ultraviolet radiation rays from the sun. This process is known as photo degradation. The polymer chains become weak from the sun's radiation and eventually become brittle and crack. This turns a plastic bag into microscopic synthetic granules that never fully decompose, which leaves their leftover remnants in landfills.

If California were to follow San Luis Obispo and ban the use of plastic bags, we could save millions of dollars, countless lives, and improve our environment. Please sign my petition to our Governor asking him to vote yes on the Statewide Plastic Bag Ban. We all can make a difference!

> Can you identify the thesis in this speech? Does the speaker sound like an authority on the topic? Is she credible? What could be added to the speech to make it easier to follow and more persuasive? What would you do differently?
>
> Used with Permission, minor parts and emphasis was added.

CONCLUSION

Persuasive speaking takes preparation and research. Use your terrific college library website as a starting point to conducting research. There are numerous guides and helpful tips on there. Remember, the first step is to find out what the CURRENT policy is and then decide how it should be changed. If you don't feel it should be changed, you will have a very difficult time coming up with a persuasive speech. In debate, you don't get to pick the side you advocate. It is chosen randomly for you. In persuasive speaking, you may need to give a speech on the side of an issue that you DO NOT agree with. Lawyers do it all the time. Don't get too connected to the issue. You must be able to be objective to succeed at this assignment.

REFERENCES

Ehninger, D., Monroe, A. H., & Gronbeck, B. E. (1978). *Principles and types of speech communication* (8th ed.).

Petty, R. E., & Cacioppo, J. T. (1981). *Attitudes and persuasion: Classic and contemporary approaches.* Dubuque, IA: W. C. Brown.

Staff (2011). *The Oprah effect: Closing the book on Oprah's book club.* Accessed from www.nielsen.com July 16, 2013.

Chapter 13

Small Group Communication

*Never doubt that a small group of thoughtful, committed
citizens can change the world. Indeed, it is the
only thing that ever has.*
—Margaret Mead

Key Concepts to Understand

What is a Small Group?
Why We Work in Groups
Advantages and Disadvantages of Groups
Types of Groups
Task versus Social Dimensions
Group versus Individual Goals
Stages of Groups
Group Norms
Roles of Group Members

Chances are that by the time you are in college, you have worked with many small groups in your academic, work, and social lives. Think about all of the groups of which you are now a member. Are you currently or have you ever been a part of: a work team, a sports team, a religious group, a family group, a social group, a study group, and of course a classroom group project/team?

WHAT IS A SMALL GROUP?

Although in our everyday conversations we tend to use the term "group" to refer to any collection of people, in this text we are going to focus on a specific type of group. To be defined as this particular type of small group, there are six characteristics that must be met.

Number of People

The definition of small group for the purpose of this text demands that we have at least three people and no more than 12. The reason there must be at least three is twofold. First, two people working together have already been defined as a dyad, and therefore are different than a small group. The reason this is different has to do with the complexity of the working relationships. If we have three people working together then there is a possibility that the group may have a majority and a minority, and that this may influence the decision-making processes (discussed in the following chapters). The reason we stop the group at 12 is simply the fact that more than 12 people are no longer a small group and will most likely have difficulty communicating with each other and sharing the decision-making process.

Communication

It should come as no surprise in this text that to be a group, the members must communicate with each other. In fact, the quality of communication (as we will discuss in subsequent chapters) influences the success of the group. However to communicate, they do not necessarily need to be in the same place at the same time. It is possible for groups to form and communicate with each other using technologies that allow dispersed mediated communication. These types of groups have now become known as Virtual Teams, people working together without actually being together.

Shared Goals

We will talk later about the delicate balance between group goals and individual's goals. For example, if you are working on a class project that involves giving a presentation in front of your class, there is a very real possibility that not everyone feels the same way about the grade they desire and are willing to work towards.

However for now, we include the notion that to become a group they must have a shared goal. Keep in mind that in the example above, the shared goal(s) can include working to present the project, but there are other goals such as earning an "A" on the final project grade that are important components of a group's goals.

Interdependent

To achieve the goals the groups have, they need to work together, share tasks, help each other, and follow through with their own commitments to be successful. This is an example of how those people are *interdependent* within that group. Most of us have had experiences working in groups where one individual's failure has affected the entire group. We know that to be successful, everyone (usually) needs to contribute his or her "fair share" of the work.

Roles

As we will explore in a subsequent section, members of groups take on various roles, some by choice and others without even realizing that they are doing so. In addition to the common roles that you may be familiar with such as a leader or note taker, there are many others that we will encounter within groups.

Identity

As a member of a group, people will begin to identify with that group in an effort to distinguish in-group membership from out-group membership. One of the ways that people do this is by naming their group. If you have seen the film *The Breakfast Club*, you may recall at the end of the film they give themselves that name.

WHY WE WORK IN GROUPS

There are numerous theories about why human beings form groups and seek to accomplish tasks in this fashion. For as far as human history has been documented, there are records of people working together in groups. The newest research suggests that our brains may not only in fact be programmed to work with others in social situations, but the fear of being left out of important groups is often what guides our behaviors (Hood, 2012).

Clearly, there are some advantages to working with groups. For example, we can divide up tasks and often accomplish more working together than we would have working alone. However, there is often more to it than performance. In fact, sometimes working in groups can be counterproductive. Most of us have experienced working with a group that was so busy talking that they didn't get much done. So why then do we choose to work in groups knowing the risk, and how can we determine the ideal situations for group work?

Advantages and Disadvantages of Groups

To answer this question, we first must ask it. In other words, before beginning a project with a group, it might make sense to decide if the project is ideally suited to working with a group or if we would be more productive working alone. Then we must ask another question that is often neglected: Is the social element of the group going to be an advantage or a disadvantage?

There are several advantages to working in groups that go beyond just getting more work done (although that is often one of them). Research shows that groups tend to perform better than individuals on many types of tasks such as community service work. People report higher satisfaction working with groups on social projects. Additionally, people say that they often learn more and become more creative working with groups (see Frey, 2002).

An incredible example of this is the recently opened Center for Innovations in Learning at Stanford University. The center teaches graduate students from all majors how to work together and develop creative ideas. It is based on the principals of David Kelley, the CEO and founder of IDEO in the Silicon Valley. Some of the things this company has invented include the computer mouse, the early version of a smartphone, and the thumbs up/down button on your TiVo, just to name a few. The program emphasizes working together in creative ways to come up with ideas that solve problems for people. And it is something that would never have been accomplished without creative people working together in groups—collaborating, brainstorming, and sharing ideas (see: http://www.ideo.com/work/stanford-center-for-innovations-in-learning/).

There are, of course, some disadvantages to group work. They include the obvious such as taking more time, having to deal with conflicts, and the inevitable problems with group members' lack of equal participation. As we will see later in this chapter, there are some useful strategies for dealing with many of these disadvantages.

TASK VERSUS SOCIAL DIMENSIONS

Every person who is part of a group and every group as a whole have the distinct challenge of balancing the work that needs to get done with the relationships between members of that group. These two dimensions of group life require a delicate balance for a group to be effective and successful. On one hand, the group has a **task** to accomplish. This is the work, or project, or reason that this group has come together in the first place. On the other hand is the **social** element of maintaining working relationships with others that requires they get along. The most successful groups are the ones that find this balance early on and are able to focus on both dimensions, without putting too much effort into one over the other. As we will see in the next chapter, when this does not happen, when this balance is not found, the group is less likely to be successful. If groups are too worried about getting along, they can often make poor decisions and are unlikely to find the best possible solution. However, if they focus too much on the task at hand, group members are less satisfied with the group and tend to dislike working together.

Types of Groups

If you completed the activity in the opening of the chapter and identified all of the various groups of which you are a member, you probably have quite a few. Let's now look at the specific types of groups we can be members of and the unique goals and purposes each of these entails (Engleberg & Wynn, 2010):

Primary groups provide members with love, support, and a sense of belonging. These include family groups and close groups of friends. Examples could include your own family or your tight-knit peer groups (I believe young people refer to them as their "homeys" or their "crew.").

Social groups share common interests and engage in social activities together. These include hobby groups, casual sports groups, or peer groups. Examples could include a model airplane group, a hiking club, or a couple of guys who meet to play basketball every Tuesday afternoon.

Self-Help groups are organized to support and assist each other in dealing with or getting past some personal problems. These can include therapy groups and weight loss groups. Examples could include Alcoholics Anonymous, Weight Watchers, or single parent groups.

Learning groups help members to study together, learn new ideas, and share knowledge. These can include informal study groups from class (however, not the same as a class project that is a work group), bible study, and book clubs. Examples would be Communication Class study group, Men's Bible Study, or 50 Shades of Grey ladies book club.

Service groups meet with the purpose of volunteering outside of the group and supporting charitable causes. These can include church groups, national or local service groups, or charitable foundations. These groups often meet together but then organize outside volunteer work at local shelters, schools, or community parks. Examples include Kiwanis Clubs, Police Activity Leagues, and environmental nonprofit groups.

Civic groups support causes within the groups. So rather than go outside of the group to volunteer, these groups do their charity work for and within the actual group. These can include school groups, professional associations, and neighborhood groups. Examples include the PTA (parent/teachers association), California Teachers Association, Neighborhood Watch Groups, or Habitat for Humanity.

Work groups are organized and exist to achieve specific tasks for the organizations or businesses the members work for. There are two broad types of these groups: Committees and Work Teams.

Committees are groups that are most often organized in the workplace and given a task of solving a problem or accomplishing some specific task such as organizing a holiday party, retirement dinner, or increasing sales. There are three types of committees:

> *Ad hoc* committees are created for a specific task and then are disbanded after the task is completed. This could be a group organized to plan the 50th anniversary party of a bank.
>
> *Standing* committees have an ongoing and active task. This could be the group organized to plan and throw the annual holiday party in the workplace.
>
> *Task force* gathers information and then is asked to make recommendations to those in positions of authority or leadership. This

could be a group that was organized to survey employees and find out what they feel would improve the workplace and then report those findings to the CEO.

Work Teams are the second type of group that is organized within the workplace or other organizations. These are typically ongoing groups, unlike committees, which are either temporary or at least meet only certain times of the year. These groups also meet for the purpose of accomplishing the work of the organization. Examples could include a legal team that includes several different lawyers with different specializations (taxes, employee law, and patents), legal assistants, and administrative assistants. Or a design team made up of engineers, artists, accountants, and legal experts.

Public groups meet for the purpose of improving issues that affect the public communities. These meetings most often take place in public where community members can come and listen and/or participate or comment on issues, concerns, and suggestions. These types of meetings can be organized into any of four categories.

Panel Discussions involve people sitting on a panel interacting with each other and discussing topics that each has a role in or knowledge of. The goal is to educate the audience. These are very common on television talk shows and on university campuses as well.

Symposiums involve a group of people who take turns speaking and making short presentations. Here the members are not interacting with each other but instead taking turns giving speeches. These are very common at academic conferences, in college settings, and even in community meetings. An example of a symposium would be three different professors from three different colleges talking about their research in front of an audience.

Forums are similar to the above but add the ability for audience members to participate, ask questions, and express opinions. These usually require a moderator (although often moderated by a member of the panel) who can limit time at the microphone. These are very common in city council or town hall meetings where they allow community members to step up to the microphone and ask questions of the panel members.

Governance Groups meet to make decisions usually in front of the public (although occasionally retreating to closed door sessions) but without the input of the public and without the goal of educating the public as panels and symposiums do. These can include the Associated Student Body or the Academic Senate (a group of faculty who make decisions about educational requirements, faculty working conditions, and other important issues at a college).

As you can imagine, some groups (such as a city council boards) may at different times act in different capacities and could be considered more than one of the above types of groups depending on the time we are looking at them.

GROUP VERSUS INDIVIDUAL GOALS

Although there is an old cliché that "there is no *I* in team" (meaning that to be a successful team the members are required to put personal needs aside and focus on the betterment of the team), the reality is that people often join groups for personal reasons and with personal goals in mind. As a result, groups are constantly in flux with balancing the goal of the group and the goals of the individual members.

Although some people bring personal goals to the group, not everyone does. There are times that people (often because they are required to join the group) don't really have any goals, and in fact just don't care. Most of us have experienced working in groups where members really were not involved, didn't do their share of the project, and seemed not to care about the group at all.

Successful teams understand this and allow group members to share personal goals that they bring to the team, striving to balance those goals with the goals of the group. For example, in classroom group projects it often makes sense to discuss the grade people would like to earn on the project as well as the reasonable time commitment available to complete it (it's easy for someone to say they want an "A," but the truth is that person really does not want to meet on the weekends to work on the project because they like to sleep in late).

STAGES OF GROUPS

In the 1950s, social science research on group work exploded with dozens of researchers studying what made groups effective in the workplace. The result of that fruitful research is that there are now dozens of theories of what makes groups successful (Frey, 2002). However, one popular model of group behavior suggests that groups go through some distinct stages in their development (Tuckman, 1965). In fact this is so popular, chances are if you search online for the topic you will find hundreds of websites dedicated to these stages. These stages seem to apply more to the types of groups people will work with during a class project, and especially when the members have not been friends with each other prior to starting the group. The stages are:

1. **Forming**
   This is the stage where people first join the group. It is characterized by communication about getting to know each other and people tend to be very reserved and hold back in sharing opinions and ideas out of concern for getting to know each other, getting along, and making a good impression.

2. **Storming**
   In the second stage of storming, group members have started to get to know each other and begun work on their project or task. As a result, there is often conflict that emerges as the group tries to get down to business and focus on completing the task. Additionally, group members will have often settled into certain roles (see next section) and competition surfaces for things like leadership and participation.

3. **Norming**
   Once a group finds their "rhythm" and begins working well together, they have entered the norming stage. Usually by this point, they have resolved their initial conflicts and found a way to work effectively together. Now communication becomes more open and direct and group members are able to criticize each other without the repercussions of the storming stage. Members are able to focus on task completion and still work well together.

4. **Performing**
   When the group reaches this stage, the members are in the process of completing their task and achieving a common goal. By now, the group members have often developed identity with the group and loyalty to other group members, along with a shared sense of ownership of the task at hand. They are focused on completing the project, but also on working well together as a team. They have usually resolved and managed conflict and are able to minimize tension within the group.

In later years, a fifth stage was added to recognize that many groups are temporarily assigned tasks and will have to dissolve at some point after the project is completed.

5. **Adjourning**
   This is where the group must now part ways. It can lead to sadness and a desire to remain in contact (this has been called *mourning* also). Some groups will attempt to continue to work together or even plan reunions in the future. Others will just go their separate ways and say their goodbyes without plans to meet again.

GROUP NORMS

When people become members of groups it is common for them to establish **norms**, or commonly accepted ways of behaving within the group. Sometimes these can be formally decided upon, and even written out **(explicit)** but there are also informal, unspecified norms that develop as well **(implicit)**. An example of an explicit norm would be when someone in the group says, "Let's all agree to text each other if we are going to be late for a meeting." An example of an unstated and implicit norm is the feeling you have that if you are going to be late you *should* text the group and let them know because it's the right thing to do.

As members of groups, we often feel implicit pressure to conform to the norms of the group. One famous example of this occurred in the 1970s at Stanford University when Philip Zimbardo created a realistic-looking prison in the basement of one of the buildings. Students were randomly chosen to be prisoners or guards. Within a short time, the guards became abusive towards the prisoners and the prisoners became complacent toward the guards' demands. Dr. Zimbardo cancelled the experiment early because it had gotten out of control.

If you are studying communication, business, anthropology, sociology, psychology, or anything that addresses the issues of group conformity, I highly suggest that you look for the videos of these experiments online. They are fascinating examples of the power group memberships have over our personal decision-making processes.

ROLES OF GROUP MEMBERS

In addition to balancing task and social dimensions, dealing with the power of conforming to group norms, and trying to get along with group members, we assume roles within our groups and oftentimes we don't even realize that we have that are sometimes done without even realizing that we are doing it.

Over 60 years ago, two researchers identified a number of different roles (some effective, some not so effective) that they found people assume in groups. In the years since, this list has been modified and expanded. However, despite its age the list serves as a valuable way of categorizing individual's roles within their groups (Benne & Sheats, 1948).

Task Roles

These are the roles that relate to getting the work done. They represent the different roles needed to take a project step-by-step from initial conception through to action.

Initiator/Contributor – Proposes original ideas or different ways of approaching group problems or goals. This role initiates discussions and moves groups into new areas of exploration.

Information Seeker – Requests clarification of comments in terms of their factual adequacy. Seeks expert information or facts relevant to the problem. Determines what information is missing and needs to be found before moving forward.

Information Giver – Provides factual information to the group. Is seen as an authority on the subject and relates own experience when relevant.

Opinion Seeker – Asks for clarification of the values, attitudes, and opinions of group members. Checks to make sure different perspectives are given.

Opinion Giver – Expresses his or her own opinions and beliefs about the subject being discussed. Often states opinions in terms of what the group "should" do.

Elaborator – Takes other people's initial ideas and builds on them with examples, relevant facts, and data. Also looks at the consequences of proposed ideas and actions.

Coordinator – Identifies and explains the relationships between ideas. May pull together a few different ideas and make them cohesive.

Orienter – Reviews and clarifies the group's position. Provides a summary of what has been accomplished, notes where the group has veered off-course, and suggests how to get back on target.

Evaluator/Critic – Evaluates proposals against a predetermined or objective standard. Assesses the reasonableness of a proposal and looks at whether it is fact-based and manageable as a solution.

Energizer – Concentrates the group's energy on forward movement. Challenges and stimulates the group to take further action.

Procedural Technician – Facilitates group discussion by taking care of logistical concerns like where meetings are to take place and what supplies are needed for each meeting.

Recorder – Acts as the secretary or minute-keeper. Records ideas and keeps track of what goes on at each meeting.

Personal and/or Social Roles

These roles contribute to the positive functioning of the group.

Encourager – Affirms, supports, and praises the efforts of fellow group members. Demonstrates warmth and provides a positive attitude in meetings.

Harmonizer – Conciliates differences between individuals. Seeks ways to reduce tension and diffuse a situation by providing further explanations or using humor.

Compromiser – Offers to change his or her position for the good of the group. Willing to yield position or meet others half way.

Gatekeeper/Expediter – Regulates the flow of communication. Makes sure all members have a chance to express themselves by encouraging the shy and quiet members to contribute their ideas. Limits those who dominate the conversation and may suggest group rules or standards that ensure everyone gets a chance to speak up.

Observer/Commentator – Provides feedback to the group about how it is functioning. Often seen when a group wants to set, evaluate, or change its standards and processes.

Follower – Accepts what others say and decide even though he or she has not contributed to the decision or expressed own thoughts. Seen as a listener not a contributor.

Dysfunctional and/or Individualistic Roles

These roles disrupt group progress and weaken its cohesion.

Aggressor – Makes personal attacks using belittling and insulting comments. Actions are usually an attempt to decrease another member's status.

Blocker – Opposes every idea or opinion that is put forward and yet refuses to make own suggestions. The result is that the group stalls because it can't get past the resistance.

Recognition Seeker – Uses group meetings to draw personal attention to himself or herself. May brag about past accomplishments or relay irrelevant stories that paint him or her in a positive light. Sometimes pulls crazy stunts to attract attention like acting silly, making excess noise, or otherwise directing members away from the task at hand.

Self-confessor – Uses the group meetings as an avenue to disclose personal feelings and issues. Tries to slip these comments in under the guise of relevance. May relate group actions to his or her personal life.

Disrupter/Playboy or Playgirl – Uses group meetings as fun time and a way to get out of real work. Distracts other people by telling jokes, playing pranks, or even reading unrelated material.

Dominator – Tries to control the conversation and dictate what people should be doing. Often exaggerates his or her knowledge and will monopolize any conversation claiming to know more about the situation and have better solutions than anybody else.

Help Seeker – Actively looks for sympathy by expressing feelings of inadequacy. Acts helpless, self-deprecating, and unable to contribute.

Special Interest Pleader – Makes suggestions based on what others would think or feel. Avoids revealing his or her own biases or opinions by using a stereotypical position instead.

SUMMARY

Working in groups is a ubiquitous part of our lives and will probably continue to become more influential as we age. We always experience the challenge of balancing the task at hand with the social relationships between group members. When things work out well, our groups are able to progress reasonably and come up with a successful outcome that all members share ownership of and feel satisfied completing.

REFERENCES

Benne, K. D., & Sheats, P. (1948). Functional roles of group members. *Journal of Social Issues, 4*, 41–49.

Hood, B. (2012). *The self-illusion: How the social brain creates identity.* New York, NY: Oxford.

Engleberg, I. N., & Wynn, D. R. (2010). *Working in groups* (5th ed.). Boston, MA: Allyn & Bacon.

Frey, L. R. (2002). *New directions in group communication.* Thousand Oaks, CA: Sage.

Tuckman, B. W. (1965). Developmental sequence in small groups. *Psychological Bulletin, 63*, 384–399.

Chapter 14

Conflict and Cohesion in Groups

Indifference and neglect often do much more damage than outright dislike
—J. K. Rowling
Harry Potter and the Order of the Phoenix

Key Concepts to Understand
What is Conflict?
Types of Conflict
Conflict Styles
Cohesion
Groupthink

In January of 1986, just over a minute after takeoff, the space shuttle Challenger exploded on live television. In a cloud of smoke, the crew compartment fell back to earth. All seven of the crew members on board perished in the accident including Christa McAuliffe, a schoolteacher from New Hampshire who had been selected from a nationwide search to join the astronauts as the first teacher in space. In the months that followed, the investigation shed light on some poor decision making by NASA officials that clearly influenced the demise of the rocket. The day the shuttle was launched was the third attempt. Two previous attempts had been scrubbed due to mechanical concerns. Reports found that the day of the launch was so cold that there were icicles on the shuttle. The engineers who made the solid rocket booster told NASA that it was too cold to launch the rocket, but officials disregarded that information. When investigating the construction of the space shuttle, paperwork showed there were problems with fitting the parts together, yet for some reason the head managers at NASA may not have been told about these problems. The reports found that there were some communication breakdowns, some conflict, some poor decision making, and some pressure to launch the shuttle into space as soon as possible. This tragedy has since been used as an example of communication failures by those studying engineering, business, psychology, and of course communication.

WHAT IS CONFLICT?

When we think of conflict, we tend to think of it as something negative that leads groups to disagreements and sometimes fighting. However, conflict doesn't have to be a bad thing for a group. In fact, chances are most groups will experience *some* conflict during the process of working on their task. The difference between success and problems has more to do with how the group handles the conflict rather than if they have conflict at all.

Conflict is simply disagreements and disharmony that occurs between people as a result of different ideas, goals, values, and behaviors. As you can see, if we define conflict this way, it is often inevitable.

Types of Conflict

There are three primary areas or types of conflict that we can see arise anytime people come together to work on a project or share a goal (Putnam, 1986):

Substantive conflict occurs when we have disagreements over the ideas, decisions, actions, or goals of the group. An example of substantive conflict is when the group is having conflict over what to do for their class project.

Affective conflict occurs when the group members are disagreeing over the personalities, communication styles, or values and beliefs of the group. Sometimes this is thought of as interpersonal conflict between members. An example of affective conflict is when certain members feel that they are not liked by the group, or feel some group members are trying to take too much power and control over the group.

Procedural conflict occurs when the group members disagree over how to run meetings, plan activities, or move towards making a decision. This is conflict over *how* to get things done. An example of procedural conflict is when some group members want to brainstorm ideas first, and others think that they should just vote on an idea.

Conflict Styles

As you have probably experienced, people tend to have certain ways they are likely to respond to conflict. Although there are certainly factors that influence how much we will be willing to work on the conflict to try and get past it and or resolve it, research shows that people typically have a dominant conflict management style that they use. For example, do you know someone who seems to constantly be competitive and tries to win every chance possible? Thomas and Kilmann (1977) identified five distinct conflict styles listed below.

Avoidance
Some people lean towards a conflict avoidance style and would rather not engage in any conflict. Someone using this style may try to change the subject to avoid conflict, and if that doesn't work may just walk away from any conflict they experience between group members.

Accommodation
Some people tend to give in to conflict even if it means that their own goals or needs are not met. This style reflects a genuine desire to get along with the group.

Competition
Some people will use a competitive style in a desire to gain the upper hand in arguments, show their superiority, be right, and feel that they are the winner.

Compromise
When someone is using the compromising conflict style, they are not giving in (accommodation) but they are expecting both sides to give in

to some degree. This can be thought of as the middle ground (or meeting halfway) in conflict resolution.

Collaboration

If both parties are able to walk away from the conflict feeling that they did not have to give in or meet in the middle, and yet still got something they wanted, then the collaboration style has been used. Using this conflict resolution style means all parties feel they have won (the term "win-win" applies here).

As you can imagine, there are certain times that each style may be ideal, and other times that a particular style may be unrealistic. If we examine how each style differs on the concern for self and concern for others, we can arrange the conflict styles on the chart below.

Figure 13.1 Conflict Styles and Concern for Parties Involved

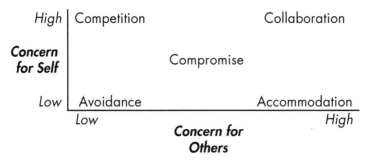

So, if you know that the conflict could erupt into violence, it may make perfect sense to completely avoid engaging the other party. By the same token, there may be times that both parties' needs are so polar opposite that collaboration would be impossible, and the best we can hope for is a compromise. And finally there are some times that competition can be appropriate (such as in sports). So the point to take away from this section is that while collaboration is an *ideal* style it is not the *only* ideal style in *every* situation.

COHESION

When group members do get along, like each other, and work well together, we can say that the group is experiencing **cohesion**. Highly cohesive groups can often be the most enjoyable to work with and members report more satisfaction with cohesive groups than with groups that don't get along. That is because cohesive groups tend to get along well by communicating in ways that show friendliness and support for each other. This is what is often called a positive communication climate. Additionally in cohesive groups, members feel a strong desire to conform to group expectations and avoid causing conflict. All of this is usually a good thing, however, there are some risks to having "too much" cohesion.

If the group is so focused on getting along and avoiding conflict, there becomes a strong risk that they will not consider a multitude of alternatives and not spend time discussing and even debating possible solutions, outcomes, and goals. Members who may see potential problems are unlikely to speak up for fear that they will upset the cohesion in the group. Obviously, these may not be good situations for a group that has to make some big decisions with important consequences.

GROUPTHINK

In 1972, the late Irving Janis, a psychologist from Yale University, published a book based on his research about a phenomenon he called "**groupthink**." Groupthink occurs when highly cohesive groups are so focused on reaching consensus and getting along that they avoid any disagreement and will fail to explore alternatives even when they have information that they are making a bad decision. His research examined some U.S. foreign policy fiascos that lead to tragic consequences such as the attack on Pearl Harbor, the Korean War, and the escalation of the Vietnam War (Janis, 1972).

In fact, when Dr. Janis examined what went wrong in the space shuttle Challenger disaster, he found some startling discoveries that shed light on how important it really is for groups to avoid becoming *too* cohesive (Griffin, 1997).

There are eight characteristics that often lead to groupthink according to Janis, and although they are not necessarily causes of the problem, they are symptoms of it. Meaning, just because a group does these things doesn't mean it will cause them to fall victims of groupthink, but when we look at groups that have made poor decisions because of groupthink, we will see many of these eight symptoms.

1. **Invulnerability.** Group members think that they are always going to be right and will take big risks out of overconfidence. Janis found that NASA had developed an attitude of "immunity from danger." The leaders thought they were just too big and too smart for anything to go wrong.

2. **Rationalization.** Group members will make excuses about any contradictory information and discount or even neglect it. Janis found this when NASA managers told the engineers not to worry about the cold weather and went ahead with the launch.

3. **Morality.** Oftentimes the group will ignore the moral or ethical consequences of their actions. Janis found this when he studied the Watergate break-in during the Nixon administration.

4. **Stereotyping Outsiders.** Group members consider anyone who is not part of their group to be weak, unintelligent, and incapable of being any sort of threat to the group and what it represents. Janis found this in studying the Vietnam War. Political leaders thought the pro-communist Vietnamese fighters were not a real threat to American soldiers.

5. **Self-Censorship.** Sometimes group members will develop a climate of censorship so that anyone even within the group who disagrees will avoid speaking up. More recent research in addition to what Janis found in studying the attack on Pearl Harbor suggests that the United States either should have known, or may have suspected that Japan was planning an attack, yet they did not prepare as well as they should have.

6. **Pressure to Conform.** Members of the group feel that they should agree with the group, even if they don't. Janis found that there was tremendous pressure on NASA officials to hurry up and launch the space shuttle Challenger and that may have led them to make some of the other mistakes.

7. **Illusion of Unanimity.** Oftentimes in falling victim to groupthink, the leaders of the group make the faulty assumption that everyone agrees with them. This is usually a result of number 5, since the group has self-censored and no one has said they disagree; leaders assume this to be the case. In fact, people who do not agree have simply chosen not to speak up. Janis found this to some degree in the space shuttle accident. It appears that paperwork "bypassed" key shuttle managers that there were potential problems and the managers assumed everything was just fine.

8. **Mindguarding.** Some group members will take on the role of mindguards, shielding the group from adverse members or information. They may even fool members into avoiding meetings just so they won't speak up against the group. It is unclear if this happened in the space shuttle disaster, but for

some reason managers were not given important information about safety concerns.

Preventing Groupthink

Janis has suggested several great ideas to avoid falling victim to groupthink. Clearly being aware of the potential for groupthink is the first step, but here are a few more useful ideas:

1. **Critical Evaluator.** Group members should take turns serving as critical evaluators, meaning they can freely bring up concerns, doubts, objections, and disagreements.

2. **Outside Experts.** Groups should bring in outside experts that do not have a stake in the decision to evaluate and critique. This reduces the stereotyping and invulnerability of the group making sure to get additional perspectives.

3. **Devil's Advocate.** Several members should be encouraged to play the devil's advocate and think about all of the things that could go wrong. This prevents that fallacy of invulnerability.

4. **Allow Multiple Channels.** Since some group members are less comfortable speaking up in public, allow the use of in-person discussions, email, and written communication that may give some members more freedom to speak up without feeling the pressure to conform that they often do in person.

5. **Encourage Secret Ballots.** If a group has anonymous or secret ballots, then people will have complete freedom to share opposing viewpoints and disagree with the group without the fear of reprimands.

SUMMARY

As you can see, some conflict in groups can be a good thing. It helps groups to weight alternatives and avoid groupthink. Although there are multiple styles of conflict resolutions, there is not necessarily one ideal style. Each has its appropriate time and place. Finally, groupthink is something that can cause major harm to groups, and when responsible for life and death decisions, can lead to harm to others as well. Yet, with knowledge and some preparation, group members can find ways to remain cohesive, get along, enjoy working with the group, and still be successful.

REFERENCES

Griffin, E. (1997). *A first look at communication theory* (5th ed.). New York, NY: McGraw-Hill.

Janis, I. L. (1972). *Victims of groupthink*. New York, NY: Houghton Mifflin.

Putnam, L. (1986). Conflict in group decision making. In R. Y. Hirokawa & M. S. Poole (Eds.), *Communication and group decision making* (pp. 175–196). Beverly Hills, CA: Sage.

Thomas, K. W., & Kilmann, R. H. (1977). Developing a forced-choice measure of conflict-handling behavior: The "MODE" instrument. *Educational and psychological measurement, 37,* 390–395.

Chapter 15

Leadership in Groups

The most dangerous leadership myth is that leaders are born—that there is a genetic factor to leadership. That's nonsense; in fact, the opposite is true. Leaders are made rather than born.

—Warren Bennis

Key Concepts to Understand

What is Leadership?
Types of Leaders
Approaches to Leadership
Leadership Theories
Leadership Styles
Leadership Models

One of the most notable leaders in American business was the co-founder of Apple Computers: Steve Jobs. Many consider him to be an example of a great business leader, a visionary man, and a pioneer in the world of new technology. An example of his exceptional ability to lead people can be seen in the story told in his biography.

When Steve Jobs returned to Apple he began taking his top 100 people on a retreat every year. At the end of their time together he would stand in front of a white board and ask his people to share the most important things they should be working on for the next year. As the employees would fight for their ideas to be written on the board, Jobs would cross off the ones he thought weren't good enough. At the end, the group would come up with the top ten. Then Steve would slash the seven at the bottom of the list and tell them they can only do three (Isaacson, 2011). As this story illustrates, one (of the many) thing Jobs excelled at was getting people to be their best, come up with great ideas, and work together to turn those ideas into goals and then to accomplish them successfully.

WHAT IS LEADERSHIP?

Leadership has been studied and debated by scholars for thousands of years. Over 2,300 years ago, Aristotle questioned why some men were born "marked" for becoming great leaders. Yet as Warren Bennis (1989), who is a business professor and highly respected authority on leadership, suggested in the opening quote of this chapter, leaders are not born that way but instead people become great leaders. So, you can see how much debate and disagreement this topic causes among great minds. Many of these scholars have defined leadership and an online search would reveal thousands of different definitions on the topic. However, for the purposes of this text, I will define **leadership** as the ability to communicate effectively to guide group members toward achieving a common goal.

Types of Leaders

There are two different types of leadership positions that we can hold. At times people may be placed into positions of leadership because of their role, job title, or even by vote. For example, if your group elects you as the leader, you would be said to be the **designated leader**, or someone who was selected by an outside power. This could include your group, your manager, or even your friends.

However, there are also times when the group doesn't necessarily choose someone to be the leader, but instead someone emerges as the group leader. An **emergent leader** is one who evolves into the position through interaction with others. Some have argued that emergent leadership is superior to designated leadership due to the fact that the person has *earned* their status. However, that is not always true. People can be designated leaders due to their success and ability to lead.

APPROACHES TO LEADERSHIP

As we have discussed so far, there is tremendous disagreement about what makes someone a great leader and where these skills come from. There is still a great deal of disagreement about what characteristics, traits, or situations make people great leaders. If you think of people whom you admire as great leaders, there is a strong possibility that you would be able to identify a list of things that they all have in common that define great leadership. Although chances are, not every leader has the same characteristics. Some leaders are great "people-persons" and others aren't so good at dealing with people. Steve Jobs was said to have been at times rude to his employees, yet many said they loved working for him (Isaacson, 2011). So, where did these characteristics come from? Were they born with them or did they learn them and develop them over time? There are four primary theories about what makes people effective leaders. Each has some very different thoughts on the subject.

Traits Leadership Theories

The ideas that leaders are born—not made—defines the majority of **trait** theories of leadership. These often include the idea that certain personality traits are what make people great leaders. As you have seen, many scholars of today don't buy into these theories. However, if you were to conduct research at a preschool, you may be surprised to see that qualities that most of us consider leadership will show up from a very young age.

Leadership Styles

In 1939, research psychologist Kurt Lewin identified three leadership styles that when used could be effective (Lewin, Lippit, & White, 1939). The researchers felt that each of these styles could be learned, and when used appropriately would yield better and more effective leaders. Each of the styles differed on how much control the leader exerted over his/her followers.

Autocratic Leadership is exhibited in someone who tries to maintain power, authority, and control over their followers. This leader will often make most of the decisions and expect the group to follow along. They often use rewards and punishment for getting people to take action.

While it may seem like this leadership style is ineffective, there may be times that it would work well. In the military, this leadership style is necessary. After reading about Steve Jobs, I think he often acted rather autocratically as CEO of Apple. Obviously it worked. When he left his position, the company was incredibility successful (Isaacson).

Democratic Leadership can be seen when someone aims for equality and shared decision making within a group. This leader is most likely to focus on both the task and the group relationships. They rely on and support the individuals in the group to participate and take ownership of the group's decisions. These leaders are usually good at listening to group members' concerns and are open in communicating with everyone. Although it may seem like this would be the preferable leadership style (and it often is), there are times when it may not be effective. It wouldn't work in the military to be democratic (imagine a sergeant asking, "Who wants to go into battle today? . . . All in favor say 'I.'" That probably would not make for a very committed or organized military).

Laissez-Faire, the third type of leadership style, comes from the French phase meaning: "let them do" as they will. Although taken from reference to government control, in leadership it refers to a leader who is hands-off and lets the groups do whatever they want on their own to achieve the goal of the group.

Situational Leadership

These theories suggest that rather than being born with a leadership trait or possessing a particular leadership style, effective leaders will use a variety of different attributes and styles depending on the situation at hand.

There are a number of very popular, successful, and profitable situational leadership models that have resulted in books, training programs, and consulting projects for their developers. A quick search online would reveal some that are free and others that you would have to pay money just to use.

All of these situational leadership theories and models have three important things in common. Leaders must spend time analyzing and understanding the people they are leading, the task they are working on, and the situation in which the process is taking place. After doing so, they must be able to adapt to each of these.

Analyze People: What are the personalities of the group? Do people get along? Are they friendly, cooperative, and supportive? Once the leader understands the dynamics of the group, she can focus on getting the group to solve any problems with any of the areas that need work.

Analyze the Task: What is the goal of the project? Are we clear about where we are going and what we are doing? How will we know if we are successful? Once the leader understands these issues and has identified any problem areas, he can lead the group to developing a clear vision and purpose in regards to the task at hand.

Analyze the Situation: What stage is the group currently in? Is this situation high-pressure on the group or do they feel relaxed? Do they have a lot of control over the situation, or are they at the mercy of their supervisors or their organization? Once the leader understands the situation, she will better be able to direct the group based on where they are currently and where they need to go in the future.

For specific examples of situational models, see Fiedler's Contingency Model of Leadership Effectiveness and Hersey-Blanchard Situational Leadership Model.

Transformational Leadership

The final philosophy **Transformational Leadership Theories** is the idea that leaders rise up to an occasion and transform themselves and their followers to accomplish something great. Some examples of these types of transformational leaders are Martin Luther King, Jr., Mahatma Gandhi, and Abraham Lincoln. What these types of leaders do—according to the theory—is use their vision, confidence, determination, and communication ability to inspire, lead, and energize their followers. Research has identified four characteristics of transformational leaders (Bass, 1998).

1. **Idealized Influence** is being a charismatic and oftentimes larger than life personality. Although most transformational leaders are thought of as humble people, they are often very vocal figures that find themselves front and center before the public and media.

2. **Inspirational Motivation** refers to the ability to communicate in a way that gets listeners to see the leader's vision. The followers feel motivated, inspired, and focused on a clear goal and direction.

3. **Intellectual Stimulation** is evidenced in a leader who seeks and values input from followers and encourages them to come up

with creative and innovative ideas. Followers feel energized and stimulated to discover and bring in new thoughts and belief systems.

4. **Individual Consideration** refers to the leader's commitment to coaching and supporting the individual followers and viewing them not as a single mass, but as unique people with unique needs. Followers feel valued for their personal contributions and specific commitments.

As you can see, there is a variety of thought on the origins of leadership abilities. While some argue great leaders are born with inherent skills and traits that make people great leaders, others believe great leaders are those who rise up to the occasion and emerge as leaders, visionaries, and influencers.

LEADERSHIP MODELS

Next, we turn to several models with differing perspectives on how individuals can lead groups and teams. There are dozens (if not hundreds) of leadership models suggesting the "best" way to be a great leader. Try conducting an online search for "leadership model" and you will find numerous, colorful charts and graphs highlighting the steps to leadership success by everyone from business professionals, communication scholars, and webpage authors. It seems everyone has his or her very own theory of leadership. For this text, I will look again at Warren Bennis (1989) who offers a straightforward approach to leadership with the three basic ingredients of leadership.

1. **Guiding Vision**
   Being an effective leader means that you must have a guiding vision that directs you towards your own goals, and that you share with your group of followers so that they too can see and understand that vision.

2. **Passion**
   It should come as little surprise that another characteristic of great leadership involves the passion that the leader has and shows. One must truly love what he or she does and be able to share that passion with those group members involved in the cause.

3. **Integrity**
   Bennis suggests that to be a leader with integrity means that you possess self-knowledge, candor, and maturity. We have self-knowledge when we know our own strengths and weaknesses. We act with candor when we can be honest and straightforward with those we lead. We are mature when we understand the times we are acting on our personal beliefs or intuition versus when we are focused on analyzing the facts before us.

SUMMARY

While this summary seems like something anyone can do, one more condition of great leadership should be included. Great leaders allow mistakes, both in themselves and in others. When mistakes are made, great leaders will "own up" to them and focus on learning from them, and move forward. They see mistakes as an integral part of learning, growing, and improving. While leadership has been studied and written about extensively, especially in the context of groups and organizations, there are quite differing views on where leadership comes from, and what makes one a great leader.

REFERENCES

Bass, M. M. (1998). *Transformational leadership: Industrial, military, and educational impact.* Mahwah, NJ: Erlbaum.

Bennis, W. (1989). *On becoming a leader.* New York, NY: Basic Books.

Carless, S. A., Wearing, A. J., & Mann, L. (2000). A short measure of transformation leadership. *Journal of Business and Psychology, 14,* 389–405.

Isaacson, W. (2011). *Steve Jobs.* New York, NY: Simon & Schuster.

Lewin, K., Lippit, R., & White, R. K. (1939). Patterns of aggressive behavior in experimentally created social climates. *Journal of Social Psychology, 10,* 271–299.

Chapter 16

Problem Solving and Decision Making in Groups

In any moment of decision, the best thing you can do is the right thing. The worst thing you can do is nothing.
—Theodore Roosevelt

Key Concepts to Understand
Decision Making
Decision-Making Methods
Problem Solving
Brainstorming
Group Planning Strategy

On April 13, 1970, crew members aboard Apollo 13 discovered that there was a problem with the oxygen tank installed in their spacecraft. As a result, the astronauts were forced to abort their mission to land on the moon and instead focus on safely returning to earth. However, given the damage to the vehicle, they were unable to operate using the normal landing procedures for which they had been trained. Ground controllers in Houston faced a formidable task. They needed to develop completely new landing procedures for the now limited functions of the space vehicle, test them, and then deliver these instructions to the crew up in space. Generally, these procedures would be developed in three months. However, due to the extreme circumstances, flight control engineers were able to complete this task in only three days. As a result of this incredible problem solving under pressure by NASA engineers, the crew was able to return safely to earth (Kennedy Space Center).

THE BENEFIT OF GROUPS

As was discussed in Chapter 12, there can be some real benefits to working together with a group of people to make a decision or solve a problem. We have the benefit of multiple ideas, perspectives, experiences, and opinions. However, we also may often have the burden of multiple ideas, perspectives, experiences, and opinions. Yet, in organizations today, teamwork seems to be the prevailing way in which people are obligated to work together and accomplish tasks. Think about all of the different tasks that you have (and will) work on with a group of people. This could include a class project, student government, workplace, a jury, volunteer projects, and even social activities. Chances are you regularly find yourself working together with groups. Most of the tasks you are involved in can be divided into two categories: decision making and problem solving.

PROBLEM SOLVING AND DECISION MAKING

Problem solving and decision making are different sides of the same coin. When people in groups come together to achieve a goal and accomplish a task, they are most likely focused on one or both of these.

Decision Making

It involves making a judgment from a choice of multiple options. An example of this is when a jury must decide if someone is guilty beyond a reasonable doubt. Other examples could include a hiring committee choosing whom they will offer the job from between three candidates. Another example of decision making would be a group of the senior class student council who must decide when and where the senior prom should take place.

Problem Solving

This is a process of analyzing a situation and developing a plan to improve it. An example of problem solving can be seen in the opening of the chapter when NASA engineers on ground control had to figure out how to land the Apollo 13 spacecraft using only the equipment that was currently on board (I recommend that you watch the movie with Tom Hanks for more details about how they accomplished this task). Other examples could be figuring out how to increase sales and make more money for a business, increase the number of students applying to our college, or reduce crime in our neighborhoods. First, we will look at the process of decision making and then problem solving.

DECISION-MAKING APPROACHES/TECHNIQUES

Although there are many ways that groups can make decisions, there seems to be some common factors involved in the process that are visible when studying groups. The best decisions are likely to be made when there is good communication between group members (Gouran & Hirokawa, 1996) and when the group is able to focus on the task, needs, and purpose of the situation at hand.

Voting

Many groups naturally default to voting as a quick and easy decision-making approach because growing up in a democratic society we are installed with the belief that everyone gets a vote. However, there are times that it may or may not be the ideal approach. Voting can lead to a majority whereby the decision is accepted when more than 50% of the group members support it. Another option that suggests more agreement among group members is to set the "pass" rate at a two-thirds vote. The advantages to voting are how quick it is, so if the group is in a hurry this can be a good option. Some groups may also require voting because of the by-laws of the organization. The downside to voting is that unless the vote is 100%–0, there are bound to be group members who do not agree with the decision.

Consensus

Another way to reach a decision is by consensus where all members accept the final decision and agree to support it. Although not all members may necessarily agree with the decision, they are willing to "buy into" it and support the group in achieving a common goal. Consensus works best in groups where members have equal power and there is a positive and supportive environment. It is not effective in groups where there is strong leadership or only certain members have more power or authority over others.

Authority

The third way to reach a decision is by use of authority rule, whereby a single group member, or several group members, or even another group makes the ultimate decision. An example of this approach occurred recently in my department. The college was to hire a new professor and the hiring committee wanted input from all faculty members, although the committee would make the ultimate decision. This approach can have negative consequences on a group if the members feel the authority ignored their input or made a decision that goes against the group as a whole. However, there are times that groups may not have the final say and this can be the best option for decision making.

PROBLEM SOLVING

The primary reason most of us work in groups is to collaborate with others on complex tasks and solve multifaceted problems. So it should come as no surprise that research has been focused on this process for over 50 years (Frey, 2002). Most of that research has addressed the ways that groups can become more effective, efficient, and successful at problem solving. Although there are dozens or more of theories, models, and prescriptions about how to accomplish that, this text will focus on two areas that will improve any group's ability to solve problems quickly and efficiently.

BRAINSTORMING

It may surprise younger readers to learn that brainstorming was developed only sixty years ago, since so many people have heard about it in school. **Brainstorming** is a method of working in groups to generate multiple possible ideas and solutions (Osborn, 1953). Despite the popularity of this technique, group members, team leaders, and organizational managers often use it incorrectly. In fact, some may argue that

Steve Jobs did not use it correctly in the story discussed in Chapter 14. This technique is effective when participants do two things: suspend judgment of ideas until all have been written out, and the more ideas the better the ideas will be.

There are also four steps that are suggested in conducting brainstorming within a group.

1. **Focus on Quantity**
   The goal of the group should be to come up with as many ideas as they can think of and not to worry about whether or not the ideas are "good."

2. **Withhold Criticism**
   The group must avoid criticizing the ideas that are presented; this will allow group members to feel comfortable sharing ideas rather than holding back.

3. **Welcome Unusual Ideas**
   The group should encourage members to come up with wild, unusual, or even strange ideas (keep in mind number 2) because these new ways of thinking may provide and encourage more creative solutions down the road.

4. **Combine and Improve Ideas**
   Once the ideas are listed out, the group should then minimize the overlapping ideas and combine any ideas that seem to suggest the same ideas. In this stage they can still come up with new ideas as they go through the process of combing ideas.

Using the above rules will help groups to perform brainstorming most effectively. The best way for a group to conduct brainstorming is to find a quiet and private room with a large white board or chalkboard and take turns writing ideas on the board. Groups should also conduct brainstorming sessions for only one idea (or question/topic) at a time.

GROUP PLANNING STRATEGY (G.P.S.)

Although as I have discussed before, there are quite a few theories, models, and suggestions for how groups can be more effective, but since most of the readers of this text will be enrolled in communication classes and working on group projects, I will now focus on my own model (GPS) that was based on nearly 20 years of teaching and researching small group communication in the college classroom. Groups that have been tasked with doing an in-class project will find these steps useful in working together and successfully completing their class projects (Schultz, 2013).

1. **Get to Know Each Other**
   Perhaps this is obvious, but if you have just been assigned (or chosen) a group, you should spend some time getting to know each other and figuring out how you will get in contact with each other (email, phone, text, etc.). However, don't make assumptions about other group members, be sure to ask if they actually answer their cell phones, listen to voicemail, and how often do they check email. It is also useful to find out about past experience with similar projects and connections that they may have in the community. And finally, if a group is going to be traveling off campus, it may be useful to know if anyone has a vehicle and if so, how many people can fit in it.

2. **Set Goals and Preferences**
   It is unrealistic to think that everyone working on a group project will have the same goals and desires in terms of success, grades, etc. I'm sure most students have been involved with group projects with other students who just don't care at all about the project or class or even their own grades. So it is a good idea to discuss that early into the task. When groups are doing volunteer work, it is a good idea to discuss what types of work members would be comfortable doing. For example, if someone doesn't want to volunteer with children, seniors, or animals (or is allergic to cats), this should be brought up early during the project.

3. **Define the Project (Outcomes); Do Research**
   The third important step involves spending some time becoming clear about the project you are working on, and how you will define your success. Many groups skip this part and it can be detrimental to their success. It is important for a group to clearly understand what the project entails, what the goals are, and what a successful task will look like. This is often easy to do in class projects when the teacher may offer a grading matrix that you can use in preparation, or even show students examples of previous successful projects. However, in the workplace the project is often something new that does not have a model of success to follow. Successful groups will take time to define their

success and create measurable outcomes that can help them to gauge their success. Doing this will demand that the group conducts research that go beyond the current group members' areas of knowledge. For example, if you were part of a group working for a large bank and were in charge of figuring out how to get more customers, it would make sense to visit competitor banks and see how they operate (a task I was given several times when working as a bank teller in college).

4. **Brainstorm for Ideas**
We have already discussed the process of brainstorming so it should come as no surprise that successful groups utilize this skill set in their decision-making processes. Recall that effective brainstorming focuses on quantity of ideas over quality and reserves judgment until after ideas area collected.

5. **Decide on Project**
Once the group has a clear vision about success and has brainstormed for as many ideas as possible, they can then begin the process of making the decision about how to move forward on their project. As we have already discussed in decision making, groups may chose to vote, use consensus, or an authority rule. In my experience, groups that reach a consensus seem to be most committed to the project, attached to the outcomes, and the most successful. In order to reach a consensus at this point in GPS, groups must be communicating openly, honestly, and effectively. Members should be able to have a dialogue about the potential solutions along with concerns they have about those ideas. It is a good idea to review the chapter on conflict and cohesion (Chapter 13) and make sure the group is avoiding groupthink.

6. **Assign Roles/Tasks**
Only when consensus has been reached and all members agree on the project they will be moving forward with, are they ready to divide and conquer. Groups can now divide the project into a variety of tasks that need to be accomplished and (when appropriate) have sub-groups take responsibility for accomplishing these sub-projects. Oftentimes it is better for a group of say six people to split into two groups of three and take on more work, rather than to divide things six ways. Subgroups can create more accountability and support, which makes it less likely that some group members will neglect their tasks.

7. **Set a Timeline**

The final stage of GPS is one that few groups even think about doing. It is common for groups to end each meeting thinking about what to do next. However, that is the number one cause of groups getting behind schedule and struggling to stay on track. Instead, groups should "begin with the end in mind" and work backwards. For example, if our group is presenting our project on May 1, we should think about how much time we need to prepare and set a due date of completing the project at least a week ahead (April 24). Ideally, groups should begin by taking out a calendar and looking realistically at how much time they need to complete each of the major sections or parts of their project and set some deadlines for completion. Doing so will ensure the group is able to set a realistic timeline and monitor their progress along the way. Groups that do this final task tend to be the most successful.

SUMMARY

The purpose of most groups is to work together to make a decision, solve a problem, or both. The variety of ideas, experiences, and backgrounds can lead groups to accomplishing extraordinary feats. Yet, it is also one of the most challenging tasks facing human beings. However, with the skills discussed in this chapter you should now have more expertise in ways you can work with others to make more effective decisions and solve problems more creatively and effectively.

REFERENCES

Kennedy Space Center. www.science.ksc.nasa.gov

Gouran, D. S., & Hirokawa, R. Y. (1996). Functional theory and communication in decision-making and problem-solving groups. In R. Y. Hirokawa & M. S. Poole (Eds.), *Communication and group decision making* (2nd ed., pp. 55–80). Thousand Oaks, CA: Sage.

Frey, L. R. (2002). *New directions in group communication.* Thousand Oaks, CA: Sage.

Osborn, A. F. (1953). *Applied imagination.* New York, NY: Scribner.

Schultz, H. (2013, July). *Personal communication.*

Chapter 17

Group Meetings and Presentations

If you had to identify, in one word, the reason why the human race has not achieved, and never will achieve, its full potential, that word would be "meetings."
—Dave Barry

In September of 1787 after over 100 days of meetings that involved debates, deliberations, occasional outbursts, numerous arguments, several fights, many people quitting, and eventually some agreement, the Constitution of the United States was completed and signed. Sometimes meetings may seem counterproductive, difficult, and even wasteful, yet at times they can accomplish great things (DiBacco).

WHY MEET

Let me try to summarize the purpose of **meetings**: to get together and get things done. Although that seems straightforward, try searching on-line for *ineffective meetings* and you will find thousands of stories and articles on bad meetings and even more suggestions on how to make them better. In fact, meetings account for much of professionals' daily working lives. In my years of academics, it seems that there is a meeting taking place on campus every single workday. However, when not organized, planned, and structured, meetings can be a complete waste of time.

Given all of the technological options we have to communicate in this day and age, it is worth asking ourselves if the group really needs to meet. It may be the case that we can accomplish the same task via email, videoconference, or phone. However, if it seems clear that group members will benefit from being face-to-face, from sharing resources, and are *prepared* and ready to meet, calling for a meeting would be appropriate.

EFFECTIVE MEETINGS

There are five important qualities that make meetings effective, efficient, and will keep members feeling that their time in the meeting was well spent.

1. **They have a purpose**
   The most important point to holding an effective meeting is that there is a clear need for the meeting, the purpose is communicated to the group members, and everyone agrees on that purpose or goal. Without a clear goal or purpose, it will be difficult to have an effective meeting that group members feel satisfied with.

2. **They have the right people**
   There are times that groups may hold meetings and will not need everyone to attend. For example if the meeting involves a sub-group who is working on a particular project, there may not be a point to having all group members attend. Additionally, there may be times that the group could benefit from having outside people attend the meeting, such as a manager, teacher, or co-worker from another department.

3. **They have a time limit**
   While most meetings have a clearly stated start time, not all meetings have a stop time. However, for busy group members,

knowing exactly how long the meeting will last can be extremely helpful. Groups can be more effective when members have the expectation that there is a limited amount of time to accomplish their tasks.

4. **They have an appropriate location**
   Sometimes it can be convenient to hold a meeting in a local café rather than an office environment. However, there is an inherent risk that the noise and distractions will make communication and concentration difficult. If the group needs to get to know each other in a casual environment, a restaurant may be the perfect meeting location. However, if the group is practicing their presentation, it may be ineffective. Thinking carefully about what needs to be accomplished should aid the group chairperson in choosing the ideal location.

5. **They have the necessary resources**
   It goes without saying that if the purpose of the meeting is to share information, having that information at the meeting will be important. However, this requires that group members come prepared and that the group has access to resources needed (such as Internet, Wi-Fi, or a projector). Effective planning will aid the chairperson in making sure all members come with the resources and information needed and reduce the likelihood that the meeting will be adjourned and rescheduled later simply because of a lack of needed tools, equipment, or materials.

THE CULTURE OF MEETINGS

Just as groups develop their own unique cultures and norms, they also develop meeting cultures. For example, some groups will develop a culture that allows members to arrive late, and other groups will discourage this. Some groups will develop a culture of open communication, and others may choose to keep things formal and use **parliamentary procedures** where the chairperson must recognize a member and allow him/her the opportunity to speak. As a group, you will develop your own meeting culture either intentionally or not. If you begin your first meeting with the goal of establishing a particular culture, it will often persist throughout the entire project.

PLANNING MEETINGS

Although not all groups have a formally designated leader, it is still valuable for meetings to have someone leading them. The group member who serves as the meeting leader is the **chairperson** and is also responsible for providing an agenda to the group members. The **agenda** is a written plan of what will be accomplished at the upcoming meeting. It should be distributed to group members in advance with enough time for any member to comment on, or add to the agenda. The role of the chairperson is to call the meeting to order (start the meeting) and to lead the group in discussing the items on the agenda. If the group is using parliamentary procedures, the chairperson will also be responsible for directing communication between members.

The Agenda

A well-organized and prepared agenda is like a roadmap for the group to follow in conducing their meeting. It helps members focus on particular tasks and items to accomplish. It will keep members on track and on schedule. It can also serve to hold members accountable for completion of their individual responsibilities.

Although the meeting may not follow the agenda directly (depending on the formality of the group), it still serves as an effective guideline for the group. An agenda should include the following items (not necessarily in this order):

Figure 16.1 Elements of the Agenda

Date/Time	Clearly indicate the date and time the meeting will take place (don't forget a.m./p.m.). Include the start and end times.
Location	Make sure the location is known to all group members. Avoid confusing locations or provide directions.
Chairperson name	Include the name of the acting (or standing) chairperson so that members may contact him/her to add items to the agenda.
Group members names	Include the names of all group members who should attend the meeting.

Purpose	State a clearly objective, topic, and goal for the meeting to help members come prepared.
Approval of minutes	The group should have the opportunity to review the minutes from the previous meeting and approve them as accurate, or suggest changes be made by the recorder.
Items to accomplish	List out any items that need to be accomplished during the meeting and a summary of what will be discussed if possible.
Reports	Identify any individual reports that will be expected by group members or committees so that those people are prepared to speak on the progress of their activities.
Announcements	Include any information that the group needs to know, but that does not need to be discussed in the meeting. This could include reminders about upcoming holidays, events, etc.

Taking Minutes

Another critical function of effective meetings is keeping an accurate record of what occurs at each meeting and making that information available to group members. This is done by the **recorder** who is the individual in charge of taking minutes during the group meeting and sharing them with the group and other stakeholders. The **minutes** are the written record detailing what occurred at the meeting. This is then made available to group members and other stakeholders such as the manager, organization, instructor, etc. Remember that the minutes of a meeting serve as an important record of what was accomplished. In some cases, they act as public or even legal documents. In the case of some public organizations, the community has the right to see the minutes and examine what the members are doing, how they voted, and what they accomplished at their meetings.

The minutes should be a summary of what occurred, but not a word for word account of the meeting. It is important that they are clear, accurate, and understandable but also brief and direct. If the recorder is unclear about something that was said, how a vote was counted, or what to include in the minutes, she should ask the group to clarify. It may be helpful for the recorder to use the agenda as a guideline in taking minutes during the meeting. Finally, the recorder should write up the minutes immediately after the meeting (or as soon as possible) while it is still fresh in her mind. They must then be distributed to the group prior to the next meeting so that the group may approve the minutes at the next meeting. Effective minutes should include the following items:

Figure 16.2 Elements of the Minutes

Recorder name	Include the name of the individual or group member who has taken the minutes.
Date/time	Write the *scheduled* date and time of the meeting.
Location	Provide the location that the meeting was held.
Members present/absent	List out the members who were present for the meeting, and (if appropriate) any members who were absent from the meeting.
Meeting start time	Write the specific time the meeting was called to order and officially began.
Approval of minutes	The group should have the opportunity to review the minutes from the previous meeting and approve them as accurate or suggest changes be made by the recorder.
Items accomplished	Write with necessary detail the items that were discussed and accomplished. Write what specific group members said. And when votes were taken, include the record of how each member voted.
Items tabled	When items were not discussed they were *tabled*—to be addressed at a subsequent meeting. Include these items and a brief description of what was discussed.
Adjournment	Include the exact time the meeting was completed and adjourned.

GROUP PRESENTATIONS

The most successful group presentations are those where the group is able to work together and connect with the audience. Much of this text has focused on what makes an excellent speech and that certainly applies to group presentations. However, there are a few characteristics of these unique speeches that merit discussion.

Like any effective speech, the group must work together and prepare their presentation. Although many groups tend to divide up topics, it is important to coordinate the material so that there isn't overlap between speakers.

Outlines

The group should use one outline for the entire presentation and work together to assemble each individual part. I do not recommend that each presenter work on his or her own part independent of the rest of the group. In the event that someone makes a mistake, it is the responsibility of the remaining group members to make sure that the presentation material is covered.

The most important thing a group can do is practice the presentation together. The odds of integrating and sounding cohesive decrease greatly when people practice alone. Although in addition to practicing as a group, it makes sense to continue to practice on your own, but do not avoid practicing together as a group.

Delivery

There are some things that groups can do to improve delivery that are unique to the group presentation environment. Group members should think about how they will look and make sure that there is some symmetry in the clothing choices. While some groups may find it "cheesy" to wear matching outfits, at the least you should be dressed according to the other group members. It would look strange if some members wore suits and ties and other members wore shorts and t-shirts.

Unless your audience knows you very well, it is usually a good idea to introduce yourselves. Have you ever gone to a wedding and not known who was delivering the toast? Sometimes in a classroom some in the audience may forget the presenter's name. The introductions also serve as an opportunity to open the presentation with enthusiasm and charisma.

To show a strong sense of teamwork, group members should transition between speakers with a brief introduction. For example: "Now John will talk about how the group decided on this particular topic . . ." Just like transitions in an individual speech, these will help the audience to follow along and serve as an effective reminder of the next speaker's name.

When a group will be using multi media such as *PowerPoint*, it is important to coordinate the development of the slides or leave that task to just one group member. Slides should have consistent backgrounds, graphics, and fonts that are easy to follow and visible from anywhere in the room. Be sure to practice the presentation with your visuals and have a backup plan in case there are technological problems with them.

At least one group member should be in charge of keeping time during the presentation. Hopefully the group will have practiced with a stopwatch and be well aware of how long each section and each speaker should be taking. One or more group members should be aware of the time continuously and have a way to communicate to other group members if they are speaking too slowly or too quickly.

If your presentation will involve questions and answers (Q&A), the group should prepare in advance for this and determine a set amount of time dedicated to it. I find that groups have stronger presentations and more control over time if the Q&A occurs just before the conclusion, rather than after. This way the group can limit the time and end their presentation with a strong conclusion rather than with an audience member's question. Try to anticipate what questions you will be asked, but be prepared for something unexpected. It is usually better for a group to admit that they don't know an answer than to try and make something up. You can always say to your audience, "We don't know that, but we will get back to you when we have an answer."

SUMMARY

Although professionals in the workplace spend a great deal of time in meetings, they can be an important and effective way to accomplish tasks as a group. Meetings are much more effective when they are prepared for in advance and all group members have a clear understanding of the purpose of the meeting. If there is not a compelling reason to hold a meeting, it may often be better *not* to meet. Some groups will hold informal meetings and others will use formal parliamentary procedures. Regardless of the formality of the meeting, it is always beneficial to have an acting chairperson who provides an agenda and an acting recorder who takes minutes and provides them to the group. With some planning and preparation, meetings can be valuable and effective tools increasing group productivity.

REFERENCES

Dave Barry from www.davebarry.com

DiBacco, T. V. (1991). *History of the United States.* New York, NY: Houghton Mifflin.

Glossary

Accommodate   Conflict style that seeks to meet other's goals and not one's own goals.

Active Listening   We are prepared to listen, involved in the interaction, open-minded, and evaluating the message.

Ad Hoc Committees   Created for a specific task and then are disbanded after the task is completed.

Ad Hominem   A personal attack.

Adapters   These tend to be unintentional hand, arms, leg, and body movements (biting your nails).

Adjournment   The final stage of group development. Also the point at which a group meeting is completed and all members are dismissed.

Affect Displays   These are unintentional and emotional expressions that we generally have little or no control over.

Affective Conflict   Occurs when the group members are disagreeing over the personalities, communication styles, or values and beliefs of the group.

Agenda   A written plan of what will be accomplished and discussed at an upcoming group meeting.

Artifacts   Objects that members of cultures use to convey meaning.

Audience   A collection of people receiving messages from a speaker.

Audience Analysis	Understand who your audience is and what drives, motivates, inspires, and even upsets this group of people.
Authority Rule	A decision-making process whereby a single group member, or several group members, or an outside group makes the ultimate decision.
Autocratic Leadership	One who tries to maintain power, authority and control over their followers.
Avoidance	Conflict style that does not engage in conflict or collaboration.
Bandwagon	The "everybody's doing it, we should too" argument.
Brainstorming	A method of working in groups to generate multiple possible ideas and solutions.
Ceremonial Speech	The goal is not to share information (although there may be some need to provide some background information) but instead to connect on an emotional level with your audience.
Chairperson	The group member charged with leading a meeting and providing the agenda for the group.
Chronemics	The study of how members of a culture use time to exchange messages.
Chronological	Speeches where your main points follow a sequential time-line.
Clothing	In communication, the way in which we dress sends messages to others.
Cognitive Restructuring	Teaches us to re-think how we label and evaluate certain situations.
Cohesion	The state of group members when they get along, like each other, and work well together.

Collaboration	A conflict style that seeks to meet the needs of all parties.
Committees	Groups that are most often organized in the workplace and given a task of solving a problem or accomplishing some specific task.
Communicate Symbolically	Symbols are primarily letters, words and language. It is that language that is exchanged in messages, in an effort to exchange meaning.
Communication	The exchange of messages.
Communication Apprehension	A fear of speaking marked by an increase in heart rate, sweating, and nervousness.
Competition	Conflict style that seeks to meet individual needs.
Compromise	Conflict style that seeks to find a middle ground.
Conflict	Disagreements and disharmony that occurs between people as a result of different ideas, goals, values, and behaviors.
Conflict Styles	Certain ways people are likely to respond to conflict.
Connotative Meaning	The way a word makes people feel and the emotional attachment people place on the meaning of words.
Consensus	A decision-making process where all group members accept the final decision and agree to support it.
Context	The situation in which the communication takes place.
Convenience Sample	Measure some of the audience members whom I have easy access to connect with.

Critical Listening	To analyze, evaluate, judge, critique, and think about the message you are listening to.
Critical Thinking	To systematically analyze, break-apart, and understand the complexities of thoughts, concepts, and ideas.
Culture	A group of people who (among other things) share the ability to communicate. Also: A system for creating, sending, storing, and processing information.
De-intensification	Here we attempt to downplay our facial expression to show less of what we are feeling or thinking.
Decision Making	Making a judgment from a choice of multiple options.
Defective Testimony	When someone is untruthful, deceitful, or misquoted.
Democratic Leadership	Can be seen when someone aims for equality and shared decision making within a group.
Demographics	These are characteristics about our audience that we can use to generalize, summarize, and categorize people into similar groups or subgroups.
Denotative Meaning	The formal (often called dictionary) definition.
Designated Leader	Someone who is selected by an outside power.
Dynamic Language	Exciting and emotional language (the movie is a non-stop edge of your seat thrill ride).
Either-or Fallacy	This is the mistake of assuming that only one of two possibilities is the solution.
Emblems	These are gestures that have a direct verbal translation.

Emergent Leader	One who evolves into the position through interaction with others.
Ethnocentrism	Our cultural or ethnic biases (both conscious and unconscious) that occur when speakers view the world from the perspective of their own cultural group as one of superiority or idealism over other groups.
Ethos	The ethics and credibility of a speaker.
Euphemisms	Words that are commonly used and considered appropriate rather than the literal terminology (He went to the giant golf course in the sky.).
Evaluative Role	Words can be used in ways that are **positive, negative,** or **neutral**.
Ex Post Facto	After the fact.
Exchange	Communication is a two-way process.
Fallacies	Errors in reasoning.
Feedback	The response from a receiver to a sender.
Forums	Similar to symposiums but add the ability for audience members to participate, ask questions, and express opinions.
Gestures	A form of body movement that communicates a message.
Governance Groups	Meet to make decisions usually in front of the public (although occasionally retreating to closed-door sessions) but without the input of the public and without the goal of educating the public as panels and symposiums do.
Group Planning Strategy (GPS)	A seven-step model of planning that helps groups to analyze challenges, strategize problem solving, and communicate more effectively.

Groupthink	Groupthink occurs when highly cohesive groups are so focused on reaching consensus and will fail to explore alternatives even when they have information that they are making a bad decision.
Haptics	The study of touch as a form of communication.
Hasty Generalization	Making too quick a judgment with too little facts.
Hearing	Physiological process of receiving noise that is interacting with our eardrums and influencing our brains to respond.
Idealized Influence	Being a charismatic and oftentimes larger than life personality.
Illustrators	Hand and/or arm movements the show or reinforce meaning.
Inclusivity	Making sure that members of the audience feel they are included rather than excluded from the setting, the speech, and the environment.
Individual Consideration	Refers to the leader's commitment to coaching and supporting the individual followers, and viewing them not as a single mass, but as unique people with unique needs.
Informative Speech	To inform, educate, and provide the audience with new information.
Inspirational Motivation	Refers to the ability to communicate in a way that gets listeners to see the leader's vision.
Intellectual Stimulation	Evidenced in a leader who seeks and values input from followers and encourages them to come up with creative and innovative ideas.
Intensification	We intensify what we feel by letting (or sometimes without even knowing or controlling it) our faces show those feelings.

Intention	All parties have come together with the express purpose of exchanging messages.
Intercultural Intergroup	The study of communication between members of diverse groups, cultures, and ethnicities.
Interpersonal	Communication between two people who have a relationship between each other.
Intrapersonal	Communication within ourselves.
Kinesics	The study of body language as a form of communication.
Laissez-Faire Leadership	Hands-off and lets the groups do whatever they want to do, on their own, to achieve the goal of the group.
Language	A set of symbols, signs, codes, and rules used to exchange meaning.
Leadership	The ability to communicate effectively to guide group members toward achieving a common goal.
Listening	The act of hearing and then processing (thinking about) and responding to messages (noise).
Logos	Logical arguments that use evidence to support the claims.
Majority Vote	A vote in group decision making whereby more than 50% of members agree.
Masking	This is when we attempt to cover or change our facial expressions for something that is appropriate to the context.
Mass Media	The study of communication through mediated channels such as TV and Internet directed at large audiences.
Medium	The means by which a message moves between the sender and the receiver.

Meeting	A group of people getting together to get things done.
Message	Anything that we exchange during communication.
Messages	These are the symbols, which are moving between the sender and receiver.
Minutes	A permanent written account of what was accomplished at a group meeting.
Monochronic	A culture that views time as being very linear.
Monroe's Motivated Sequence	An organizational structure for persuasive speeches that helps the audience to follow along logically and understand the complex issues.
Neutralization	Hiding one's emotion by attempting to avoid showing any facial expression.
Noise	Anything that interferes with communication.
Non-Sequitur Fallacy	Non-sequential. Major and minor premise do not align.
Nonverbal Communication	Messages that people exchange beyond verbal communication.
Norms	Commonly accepted ways of behaving within the group—either explicit or implicit.
Occulesics	The study of the eyes as a form of communication.
Organizational	The study of communication with business, government, nonprofit, and other organizations.
Panel Discussions	Involve people sitting on a panel; interacting with each other and discussing topics that each has a role in or knowledge of.
Paralanguage	The nonverbal use of vocal tone, voice, and inflection.

Paraphrasing	A skill where you summarize and restate the message you have just heard someone say to you.
Parliamentary Procedures	A set of formal rules for how meetings are to be conducted. They are aimed at using fair and orderly discussion practices.
Passive Listening	Doesn't require that we pay much attention or offer much thought to the message(s) we are listening to.
Pathos	Appealing to one's sense of emotion (positive or negative).
Perception Checking	A skill used in interpersonal communication to verify understanding of a message.
Persuasion	The act of changing another's attitudes, beliefs, opinions, and/or behaviors.
Persuasive Speech	The speaker has the intention of convincing the audience to change their beliefs, ideas, thoughts, feelings, and/or actions.
Physical Space	Refers to how we use the space around our bodies.
Polychronic	A culture that doesn't place emphasis on the clock.
Post-Hoc	This is a statistical error that occurs when a correlation is misunderstood to be the same as a cause-effect relationship.
Primary Groups	Provide members with love, support, and a sense of belonging.
Problem Solving	A process of analyzing a situation and developing a plan to improve it.
Procedural Conflict	Occurs when the group members disagree over how to run meetings, plan activities, or move towards making a decision.
Proxemics	The study of the communication of space and distance.

Psychographics	Variables that examine the psychological complexities of the audience and allow speakers to better understand the motivations and feelings our audience members have about particular topics.
Public Groups	Meet for the purpose of improving issues that affect the public communities.
Public Speaking	An exchange of messages with an audience.
Receiver	The listener, audience, responder, and decoder. This is the person who is doing the listening.
Recorder	The group member in charge of taking minutes during the group meeting and sharing them with the group and other stakeholders.
Red Herring	A diversion to move the audience away from the real issue.
Referential Function	We use it to refer to or point to things with labels.
Regulators	Gestures that control and influence a conversation.
Relational Function	Use of language to establish and maintain our relationships.
Representative Sample	Randomly choose people to measure and if I have access to a list of ALL audience members.
Self-Help Groups	Groups organized to support and assist each other in dealing with or getting past some personal problems.
Sender	The speaker, encoder, or source. This is the person who is doing the talking.
Shared Code	We understand what the symbols used to communicate represent.

Situational Leadership — Leaders use a variety of different attributes and styles depending on the situation at hand.

Slippery Slope — When we assume that taking the first step will lead to other steps, yet there is no logical reason to assume this.

Small Group — Three to 12 people who share a common goal, are interdependent, and communicate.

Social Dimension of Groups — Element of maintaining working relationships with others that requires they get along.

Social Groups — Share common interests and engage in social activities together.

Spatial — Speech structure of using physical space.

Standing Committees — Have an ongoing and active task.

Static Language — Language that expresses little emotion.

Statistical Fallacies — Errors in reasoning due to statistical inaccuracies.

Strong Words — Words that convey powerful emotional connections (love or hate).

Substantive Conflict — Occurs when we have disagreements over the ideas, decisions, actions, or goals of the group.

Survey — Surveys utilize questions and when written and collected efficiently, can be very quick and easy ways to get simple or detailed information from the audience.

Symbols — Something that represents something else.

Symposiums — A group of people who take turns speaking and making short presentations.

Systematic Desensitization — A treatment for many different types of fears.

Task Dimension of Groups	This is the work, or project, or reason that this group has come together in the first place.
Task Force	Gathers information and then is asked to make recommendations to those in positions of authority or leadership.
Territory	How we use our surroundings.
Topical	Organized by topics and subtopics.
Trait Leadership	The idea that leaders are born not made.
Transaction	The sending and receiving of messages.
Transformational Leadership	The idea that leaders rise up to an occasion and transform themselves and their followers to accomplish something great.
Transitions	Linkages between ideas in a speech.
Tribute Speech	Primary goal of sharing and connecting emotions with the audience and explaining why this person is worthy of praise.
Two-thirds Vote	A vote in group decision making whereby more than two-thirds of the group members agree.
Visualization	A technique used to help overcome the nervousness associated with public speaking.
Weak Words	Words that do not convey powerful emotional connections (nice, OK).

*Wishing you success in your
communication class,
your education,
and beyond.*
—JT

CPSIA information can be obtained
at www.ICGtesting.com
Printed in the USA
LVHW060901160921
697921LV00002B/3